Mediterranean
SUMMER TABLE

Mediterranean
SUMMER TABLE

**TIMELESS, VERSATILE RECIPES
FOR EVERY OCCASION & APPETITE**

KATHY KORDALIS
PHOTOGRAPHY BY MOWIE KAY

RYLAND PETERS & SMALL
LONDON • NEW YORK

Dedication
For Mum, Dad and Matthew x

Senior Designer Megan Smith
Senior Editors Abi Waters
   & Gillian Haslam
Production Manager
   Gordana Simakovic
Creative Director Leslie Harrington
Editorial Director Julia Charles

Food Stylist Kathy Kordalis
Prop Stylist Lauren Miller
Indexer Hilary Bird

First published in 2023
by Ryland Peters & Small
20–21 Jockey's Fields
London WC1R 4BW
and 341 E 116th St
New York NY 10029
www.rylandpeters.com

• British (metric) and American (imperial plus US cups) measurements are included for your convenience; however, it is important to work with one set of measurements and not alternate between the two within a recipe.
• Ovens should be preheated to the specified temperatures.
• When a recipe calls for the grated zest of citrus fruit, buy unwaxed fruit and wash well before using.
• To sterilize screw-top jars, preheat the oven to 160°/150° fan/325°F/gas 3. Wash the jars and their lids in hot soapy water then rinse but don't dry them. Remove any rubber seals, put the jars onto a baking sheet and into the oven for 10 minutes. Soak the lids in boiling water for a few minutes.

CONTENTS

INTRODUCTION

Whether you are serving up a lazy weekend brunch, hosting a last-minute al fresco lunch in the garden, throwing a summer drinks party or staging a stylish celebration dinner under the stars, the ingredients and recipes in this book will transport you to the shores of the Mediterranean wherever you find yourself. This collection of easy, versatile and elegant recipes will provide you with endless inspiration for all your summer eating occasions, and cater for every taste and appetite.

For this book, I have gathered together my most trusted and reliable Mediterranean-inspired recipes, the ones that I return to again and again, in the hope that they will become firm favourites in your repertoire too. I've included ideas for refreshing drinks with accompanying flavour-paired small bites, ideas for sharing platters to graze from at your leisure, impressive recipes that showcase the freshest fish and seafood, classic and full-flavoured meat dishes, an array of vegetable dishes and recipes that make the best use of nutritious grains and pulses. I also share with you some simple ideas for cooking with, and plating, fresh cheeses and other dairy, from feta and labneh to burrata, plus some simple recipes for homemade condiments, pickles and dressings that will add the perfect finishing touch to your dishes. Also included are some easy-yet-satisfying breads to bake, such as pita and focaccia, and of course the all-important decadent desserts and cakes.

I shine a spotlight on classic Mediterranean ingredients in essays that explore the role of seasonings such as salt, mustard and spices, as well as ancient foods such as olive oil, vinegar and honey, as these are the cornerstones of so many recipes enjoyed in the Southern European countries.

All the ingredients I have used in my recipes are easy to source in most supermarkets, delicatessens and farm shops. And remember, the beauty of Mediterranean-style food is its simplicity – you should be prepared to let your good-quality ingredients do most of the work, treat them with respect in your kitchen, then relax and share the stunning results with your friends and loved ones all summer long.

aperitivo
SMALL BITES
& drinks

BLUE CHEESE ARANCINI &
GRIDDLED OLIVES *with an amaretto sour*

A trio of taste explosions! Blue cheese, charred olives and a zingy drink. This is the perfect pre-dinner small bite and drink selection. Something really special happens to olives when they are griddled – the best type of olive to use is a large buttery type like a Halkidiki as it chars beautifully and pairs well with the blue cheese in the Arancini.

Amaretto Sour (see page 15),
   to serve

BLUE CHEESE ARANCINI
400 g/2 cups arborio rice
100 g/1⅓ cups finely grated
   Parmesan
6 eggs, lightly beaten
100 g/3½ oz. blue cheese
75 g/generous ½ cup plain/
   all-purpose flour, seasoned
100 g/1¼ cups fine dried
   breadcrumbs
vegetable oil, for deep-frying
sea salt and black pepper

GRIDDLED OLIVES
200 g/7 oz. large buttery green
   olives in brine, stoned/pitted
   and drained
2 tablespoons olive oil
1 teaspoon mixed dried herbs
pinch of dried chilli/hot red pepper
   flakes
1 garlic clove, crushed
100 g/3½ oz. semi-dried/sunblush
   tomatoes

wooden skewers

MAKES 24

Cook the rice in a large saucepan of boiling, salted water for 15 minutes or until tender, then drain well, place in a large bowl and leave to cool. Add the Parmesan, two-thirds of the eggs, season generously with salt and black pepper and stir to combine. Spread the rice mixture out on a baking sheet and refrigerate until cold.

To make the arancini, place 1 tablespoon of the chilled rice mixture in the palm of your hand and flatten with a spoon. Place ½ teaspoon of the blue cheese in the centre of the rice and gently form the rice mixture around the filling to create a ball. Transfer the arancini to a large plate. Repeat with the remaining rice mixture and blue cheese – you should make about 24 arancini.

Place the flour, remaining egg and breadcrumbs in separate bowls. Roll each arancini gently in the flour, then dip in the egg, then finally roll in the breadcrumbs. Place them on a tray and refrigerate until needed.

Heat the vegetable oil in a deep saucepan or deep-fryer to 180°C/350°F. Deep-fry the arancini in batches for 3–5 minutes or until crisp and golden brown. Drain on paper towels and serve immediately.

For the griddled olives, place all the ingredients in a bowl, except for the semi-dried tomatoes. Mix the olives with the oil and seasonings, then thread the olives on to wooden skewers, place them on a flat surface and press them with something heavy to flatten them.

Heat a griddle pan until hot. Grill the olive skewers on the hot pan, while pressing them again with something heavy. After the grill pattern is printed on the underside of the olives, turn the skewers over and press them again with the weight. Remove the olives from the skewers and transfer to a bowl with the garlic and semi-dried tomatoes. Serve with the hot arancini and an Amaretto Sour, if liked.

THYME & PARMESAN CHOUX PUFFS
with a negroni sbagliato

This is a winning flavour combination. The thyme and Parmesan choux buns can be made in advance and frozen before baking. Nothing smells nicer than pastry baking in the oven, so keep these in your freezer for impromptu drinks. The Negroni Sbagliato is a classic Campari cocktail and the perfect accompanying drink for these tasty morsels.

5 large eggs

80 g/¾ stick butter, cubed

1 teaspoon sea salt

150 g/generous 1 cup plain/
    all-purpose flour

¼ teaspoon freshly grated nutmeg

1 teaspoon mustard powder

pinch of cayenne pepper

175 g/generous 2 cups grated
    Parmesan or pecorino

4 fresh thyme sprigs, leaves picked,
    plus extra to garnish

1 teaspoon honey

milk or water, for mixing

Negroni Sbagliato (see page 14),
    to serve

MAKES ABOUT 30

Preheat the oven to 200°C fan/220°C/425°F/gas 7. Line two baking sheets with parchment paper.

Crack 4 of the eggs into a jug/pitcher and beat together. Put 250 ml/ 1 cup water, the butter and salt in a saucepan over a medium heat and bring to a simmer, stirring occasionally, to help melt the butter.

Take the pan off the heat and pour in the flour, stirring until it comes together into a paste. Put the pan back over a low heat, and stir until you have a smooth ball and the dough is starting to form a layer on the base of the pan – this should take 2–3 minutes.

Take the pan off the heat and use a stand mixer or hand beaters to beat the dough for about 5 minutes until cooled.

Beat in the 4 beaten eggs, little by little, making sure each addition is well incorporated before adding the next. Stir in the nutmeg, mustard, cayenne. thyme, honey and two-thirds of the cheese. Pipe or spoon the mixture on to the prepared baking sheets (you should get approximately 30 buns from the mixture).

Whisk together the last egg with a dash of water or milk, then brush onto the buns, sprinkle with the remaining cheese and place in the preheated oven. Reduce the oven temperature to 180°C fan/200°C/ 400°F/gas 6. Bake for 20 minutes until puffed up and golden. Remove from the oven, pierce the side of each one with a small knife and put back in the oven for 5 minutes to let the steam out, before removing and devouring while they're still warm.

These drinks are so simple and pretty to serve to your guests, whether a cocktail with a twist like the *Pomegranate Martini* or the *Berry Gin Jug* which is perfect for a crowd. All are light, delicious and look so attractive on an alfresco summer table.

Negroni sbagliato

25 ml/1 fl. oz. Campari
25 ml/1 fl. oz. sweet vermouth
ice cubes
Prosecco, to top up
twist of orange peel, to decorate

MAKES 1

Pour the Campari and sweet vermouth into a glass, add ice cubes and gently pour in the Prosecco – pouring down a bar or long spoon placed in the glass will stop the bubbles fizzing over the edge of the glass.

Stir the contents of the glass together, top up further with Prosecco if needed and garnish with the orange peel.

Amaretto sour

ice cubes
50 ml/2 fl . oz. amaretto
25 ml/1 fl. oz. lemon juice
1 teaspoon syrup from a jar
    of maraschino cherries, plus
    cherries from the jar to garnish
1 tablespoon aquafaba (brine from
    a can of chickpeas)
dash of angostura bitters
dash of bourbon

MAKES 1

Half-fill a cocktail shaker with ice
cubes and add all the ingredients.
Shake really well until the outside
of the shaker is cold.

Strain the cocktail into a glass.
Skewer a few maraschino cherries
onto a cocktail skewer and use
this to garnish the glass.

Pomegranate martini

ice cubes
30 ml/1 fl. oz. citron vodka
20 ml/4 teaspoons triple sec
juice of 1 lime
50 ml/2 fl. oz. pomegranate juice

Fill a cocktail shaker with ice
cubes. Add all the ingredients and
shake to mix. Strain the cocktail
into a martini glass.

MAKES 1

*From left: Berry Gin Jug
(see page 26), Negroni Sbagliato,
Pomegranate Martini and
Amaretto Sour.*

MANCHEGO, HAM & QUINCE JELLY
TOASTIES *with a beer cocktail*

*This Spanish-inspired toastie elevates this snack to a new level, and it's
great partnered with this fun and refreshing way to drink beer. By adding
the quince jelly, piquillo peppers and thinly sliced onions to the toastie,
you are transported to balmy Spanish nights.*

40 g/3 tablespoons butter,
   room temperature
4 thick white sourdough slices
200 g/7 oz. Manchego cheese,
   thinly sliced
70-g/2½-oz. pack of thinly sliced
   Serrano ham
jar of piquillo peppers, to serve
20 g/¾ oz. quince jelly
½ red onion, thinly sliced
handful of rocket/arugula

SERVES 2

Preheat a griddle pan to medium.

Butter the sourdough slices, then build sandwiches of cheese and ham.
Place the sandwiches on the hot griddle and press with a foil-covered
brick or weighted down with a heavy frying pan/skillet. Cook for
3–4 minutes on each side to crust and mark the bread and melt
the cheese.

Serve with quince jelly and peppers on the side, and the rocket and red
onion tucked inside the sandwich.

Beer cocktail

few handfuls of crushed ice
½ teaspoon sugar syrup
1 lemon wedge, plus 1 slice
   to garnish
150 ml/⅔ cup golden ale
150 ml/⅔ cup Prosecco
75 ml/⅓ cup Pellegrino lemonade

MAKES 1

Fill a large tall glass with a few
handfuls of crushed ice, then tip
in the sugar syrup. Squeeze the
lemon wedge over the glass to
express the oils and drop it in.
Pour in the golden ale and
Prosecco and stir to combine

Top up the drink with the
lemonade. Make a small cut in
the lemon slice and secure it onto
the rim of the glass to garnish.

ANTIPASTI PLATES *with chilled vermouth*

Nothing says fun, casual and easy than some antipasti served with a chilled vermouth. This selection of antipasti is inspired by both Italy and Spain. The Griddled Melon with Jamón is a retro classic, the Courgette and Tomato-rubbed Bread (see page 20) is so simple yet impressive and using mini potatoes with their skins on in the Patatas Bravas (see page 21) is delicious! Serving the vermouth on ice further enhances the flavours of herbs, spices, barks, flowers, seeds, roots and other botanicals, making it the perfect accompaniment.

GRIDDLED MELON *wrapped in jamón*

This is an updated classic, where a little basil has been added to the inside of the ham and then it's griddled. The flavour is further enhanced by charring both the melon and ham.

20 fresh basil leaves

1 tablespoon extra virgin olive oil, plus extra for drizzling

2 tablespoons balsamic vinegar, plus extra for drizzling

1 melon, peeled and cut into 10 wedges

10 Serrano ham slices

20 g/¾ oz. Marcona almonds, chopped

black pepper

SERVES 4–6 TO SHARE

Preheat the griddle pan to hot.

In a bowl, gently toss the basil, olive oil and balsamic vinegar until the basil is well coated. Place 2 basil leaves down, end to end, on a platter.

Lay a melon wedge on the basil. Finish by wrapping a slice of Serrano ham around the melon and the basil. Repeat for the remaining melon, to make 10 parcels.

Drizzle with olive oil, sprinkle with black pepper and griddle on each side for 1–2 minutes. Drizzle with balsamic vinegar, top with chopped almonds and serve on a platter with other antipasti (see overleaf) and chilled vermouth.

Chilled vermouth

Vermouth is a fortified wine that is flavoured with a variety of herbs and spices. It is traditionally made in two major styles: dry vermouth and sweet vermouth. Dry vermouth originates in France. Traditionally, it's used to make Martinis and is dry and floral. Sweet vermouth usually comes from Italy, is sweet, spiced, and herbal, and is used in cocktails like Manhattans and Negronis. Perfect for a chilled aperitif.

COURGETTE & TOMATO-RUBBED BREAD

So simple! This is such an easy way to share food and it can be adapted with whatever you have in your fridge. The most important element is griddling the oiled bread and rubbing it with garlic and ripe tomatoes. Then eat it as is or topped with extras!

6 mini courgettes/zucchini,
    thinly sliced lengthways
1 red onion, thinly sliced
60 ml/¼ cup extra virgin olive oil,
    plus extra for drizzling
30 ml/2 tablespoons sherry vinegar
finely grated zest and freshly
    squeezed juice of 1 lemon
2 garlic cloves, 1 finely chopped,
    plus 1 halved, for rubbing
4 thick sourdough bread slices,
    halved
1 very ripe tomato, halved
2 tablespoons coarsely torn
    fresh oregano
sea salt and black pepper
shaved Manchego cheese, to serve

SERVES 4–6 TO SHARE

Combine the sliced courgettes, sliced red onion, olive oil, sherry vinegar, lemon zest and juice and chopped garlic in a bowl. Season to taste and set aside.

Heat a griddle pan over a high heat.

Drizzle the bread with extra oil and griddle, turning once, for 2–3 minutes until toasted. Rub with the cut-side of the halved garlic clove, then rub well with the cut-side of the tomato. Season to taste.

Pile the courgette mixture on top of the toasted bread. Serve scattered with Manchego.

MINI NEW PATATAS BRAVAS

Patatas Bravas are loved by everyone, and this is such an easy version of this classic, well-loved dish (but remember to start the dish well in advance so that the flavours can infuse). Roasting the mini new potatoes in their skins and adding the sauce at the end makes for a simple and delicious sharing dish.

5 tablespoons extra virgin olive oil, plus extra for drizzling
1 small onion, chopped
2 garlic cloves, chopped
227-g/8-oz. can chopped tomatoes
1 tablespoon tomato purée/paste
2 teaspoons sweet paprika
pinch of chilli powder
pinch of sugar
800 g/1¾ lb. mini new potatoes
chopped fresh basil and rocket/arugula, to garnish

SERVES 4–6 TO SHARE

Heat the oil in a frying pan/skillet over a medium heat. Add the onion and fry for about 5 minutes until softened. Add the garlic, tomatoes, tomato purée, paprika, chilli powder and sugar and bring to the boil, stirring continuously. Simmer for 10 minutes until pulpy. Set aside for up to 24 hours for the flavours to infuse.

Preheat the oven to 180°C fan/200°C/400°F/gas mark 6.

Pat the new potatoes dry with paper towels and spread them out in one layer in a roasting pan. Drizzle with oil, season with salt and pepper and toss the potatoes so they are coated in oil and seasoning. Roast in the preheated oven for 40–50 minutes until the potatoes are crisp and golden brown.

Gently reheat the sauce in a saucepan over a low heat. Tip the potatoes into serving dishes and spoon over the sauce. Serve sprinkled with the chopped basil and rocket.

FETA BAKED IN VINE LEAVES WITH BLISTERED TOMATOES *with an ouzotini*

This is inspired by the snacks or mezedes that are served alongside an Ouzo in an ouzeri, a drinks and snacks taverna – but with a twist. The Ouzo is served in a cocktail garnished with olives and cucumber. The baked feta is semi-wrapped in vine leaves and served with blistered tomatoes. Simply take to the table with some forks and share with all.

150 g/5 oz. vine-ripened cherry
   tomatoes on the vine
1 teaspoon chilli/hot red pepper
   flakes
2 tablespoons extra virgin olive oil,
   plus extra for brushing
8 vine leaves preserved in brine,
   stems removed, rinsed
200-g/8-oz. block of feta cheese,
   cut into 4 thick slices
grated zest of 1 lemon
1 tablespoon runny honey

SERVES 4–6 TO SHARE

Preheat the oven to 180°C fan/200°C/400°C/gas 6. Line a baking sheet with non-stick baking paper.

Trim the tomatoes into bunches of 3 or 4, place them on a small baking sheet and sprinkle with chilli flakes. Drizzle with the oil, season to taste and roast for 10–15 minutes until cooked through and the skin blisters.

Meanwhile, lay 2 vine leaves slightly overlapping on a work surface, brush with a little oil, place a piece of feta on top, sprinkle with lemon zest and drizzle with honey. Loosely wrap the vine leaves around the feta to form a parcel and place on the lined baking sheet. Repeat with the other feta slices and vine leaves. Brush the parcels with oil and bake in the oven for 10–15 minutes until the feta is soft and warmed through. Serve hot with the blistered tomatoes and an Ouzotini.

Ouzotini

30 ml/1 fl. oz. ouzo
30 ml/1 fl. oz. vodka
60 ml/2 fl. oz. pineapple juice
1 tablespoon freshly squeezed
   lemon juice
1 teaspoon runny honey
ice cubes

GARNISH
1 mini cucumber, shaved
   lengthways
1 green olive, stoned/pitted

MAKES 1

Add all of the ingredients to a cocktail shaker half-filled with ice cubes and shake vigorously until well-chilled. Strain into a chilled cocktail glass and garnish with cucumber and an olive.

Serve alongside the feta baked in vine leaves.

BUTTER BEAN WHIP & CRUDITÉS PLATTER
with a florabotanica

Perfect for your vegan and vegetarian guests and all lovers of vegetables. The butter/lima-bean whip, with its citrus and garlic mix, is topped with sautéed spring onions/scallions, herbs and capers and is a flavour sensation. Arrange your vegetables and breadsticks in groups with edible flowers that can also be added to your Florabotanica – a gin-based cocktail with a botanical base, mixing rose syrup, yuzu and bitters.

400-g/14-oz. can butter/lima
   beans, drained
2 tablespoons olive oil
1 teaspoon sea salt, or to taste
1 garlic clove, crushed
freshly squeezed juice of 1 lemon
black pepper
crudités, to serve

TOPPING
2 tablespoons olive oil
2 fresh rosemary sprigs,
   leaves picked
8 fresh sage leaves
2 fresh tarragon sprigs,
   leaves picked
2 spring onions/scallions,
   finely sliced
2 teaspoons capers, drained
grated zest of 1 lemon

SERVES 4 TO SHARE

Using a food processor or stick blender, blend with the beans, oil, ½ teaspoon salt, garlic, lemon juice and pepper. Taste and add the remaining salt if necessary.

Heat the oil in a sauté pan over a medium heat. Carefully add the herbs, spring onions and capers to the hot oil and fry for 1–2 minutes until crisp. Use a slotted spoon to carefully transfer the fried topping to paper towels to drain off any excess oil, reserving the oil in the pan.

To assemble, use a spatula or the back of a spoon to spread the bean dip over a nice plate or bowl. Top with the crispy herbs and a few splashes of the infused pan oil. Sprinkle over the lemon zest and serve with crudités.

Florabotanica

60 ml/2 fl. oz. gin
15 ml/1 tablespoon yuzu juice
15 ml/1 tablespoon rose syrup
1–4 drops bitters
1 teaspoon cherry liqueur
½ egg white
edible flowers and herbs,
   to garnish

MAKES 1

Shake ingredients first without ice, then shake well a second time with ice. Strain into a short glass and fill with ice. Garnish with edible flowers.

BRIOCHE BITES WITH SMOKED TROUT
& CRÈME FRAÎCHE *with a berry gin jug*

Buttery brioche lightly toasted and topped with smoked creamy zesty trout, lightly finished with some thinly sliced preserved lemon, salmon roe and peppery rocket/arugula. Served alongside a refreshing Berry Gin Jug, this combination is perfect for a crowd and pre-lunch nibbles.

200 g/7 oz. hot-smoked trout,
    coarsely flaked
50 g/1¾ oz. crème fraîche
grated zest and freshly squeezed
    juice of 1 lemon
2 tablespoons coarsely chopped
    fresh dill
1 spring onion/scallion,
    thinly sliced
sea salt and black pepper

TOPPING
1 brioche loaf, sliced and cut
    into squares
salmon roe
rocket/arugula
1 preserved lemon, thinly sliced
    into quarters

SERVES 4 TO SHARE

Combine the trout in a bowl with the crème fraîche, lemon zest and juice, dill and spring onion. Season to taste and mix gently, then set aside.

To serve, top the brioche squares with a little of the trout mixture and salmon roe and scatter with rocket and plenty of black pepper. Top with a quartered slice of preserved lemon.

Berry gin jug

200 g/7 oz. mixed berries,
    plus extra to serve
1 lime, cut into wedges,
    plus extra to serve
200 ml/¾–1 cup dry gin
ice cubes
250 ml/1 cup fruit pressé
    (choose a light coloured one,
    such as apple or elderflower)
sparkling water, to top up
fruit, to garnish

SERVES 4

Put the blackberries and lime wedges into a small jug/pitcher and muddle together with the end of a rolling pin or wooden spoon. Add the gin and stir well.

Half fill a large jug/pitcher with ice cubes. Strain the flavoured gin into the jug, discarding the blackberry seeds and lime peel.

Top up the pitcher with the fruit pressé and sparkling water, and garnish with extra mixed berries and lime wedges.

DRESSED OYSTERS
with a Champagne cocktail

An elegant way to share champagne and oysters. Both dressings are fresh and light and delicious and are perfect with the classic Champagne cocktail, which is made with orange juice and Cognac.

12 oysters, freshly shucked
crushed ice

FENNEL MIGNONETTE
100 ml/generous ⅓ cup good-
   quality red wine vinegar
80 g/3 oz. golden shallots,
   finely chopped
1 small fennel, finely chopped

POMEGRANATE DRESSING
2 tablespoons pomegranate
   molasses
2 tablespoons red wine vinegar
2 tablespoons extra virgin olive oil
50 g/⅓ cup pomegranate seeds
1 small red onion, finely chopped
black pepper

SERVES 4–6 TO SHARE

To make the fennel mignonette, combine the red wine vinegar, shallots and fennel in a non-reactive bowl. Cover with clingfilm/plastic wrap and refrigerate until required.

For the pomegranate dressing, combine the pomegranate molasses, vinegar and oil in a bowl and mix to combine. Stir through the pomegranate seeds and onion and season to taste with black pepper.

Cover a serving platter with crushed ice and top with the oysters. Spoon a little mignonette over each and then some pomegranate dressing.

Champagne cocktail

20 ml/1¾ fl. oz. Cognac
20 ml/1¾ fl. oz. orange juice or
   other juice
10 ml/2 teaspoons freshly
   squeezed lemon juice
1 teaspoon caster/superfine sugar
Champagne or sparkling wine,
   chilled, to top up
orange twist, to serve

MAKES 1

Combine the Cognac, fruit juices and sugar in a cocktail shaker. Shake well and strain into a Champagne flute. Top up with Champagne or sparkling wine, garnish with an orange twist and serve.

ex mari
FROM THE SEA
Fish & seafood

SHRIMP SKEWERS *with romesco sauce*

The roasted romesco can be made in advance to allow the flavours to develop, so all you have to do at the last minute is griddle the bread and prawns. This makes for a very easy and impressive plate.

12 tiger prawns/jumbo shrimp,
    peeled, heads removed,
    tails intact
2 garlic cloves, crushed
2 tablespoons sherry

ROMESCO SAUCE
1 vine-ripened tomato, quartered
1 red (bell) pepper, quartered
4 garlic cloves
2 tablespoons olive oil
30 g/1 oz. crustless sourdough
    bread, coarsely torn
20 g/¾ oz. roasted hazelnuts
1½ tablespoons sherry vinegar,
    or to taste
freshly squeezed juice of ½ lemon
½ teaspoon sweet paprika
sea salt and black pepper

TO SERVE
roasted red onions or shallots
griddled sourdough
salad leaves

wooden or metal skewers

SERVES 4–6 TO SHARE

Preheat the oven to 180°C fan/200°C/400°F/gas 6.

For the roasted romesco sauce, place the tomato, pepper and garlic on a baking sheet and drizzle with 1 tablespoon of the oil, season and roast in the preheated oven for about 10 minutes until tender.

Halve or quarter the onions or shallots, depending on their size, drizzle with a little oil and roast alongside the romesco mixture.

When the romesco mixture is cool enough to handle, squeeze the garlic from their skins (and discard the skins), then transfer the roasted garlic, tomato, pepper and any pan juices to a food processor or blender. Add the bread, hazelnuts, vinegar, lemon juice and paprika and process until smooth. With the motor running, slowly add the remaining oil and blend until emulsified. Season to taste and refrigerate for at least 1 hour to allow the flavours to develop.

For the prawns, put the prawns, garlic and sherry in a bowl and refrigerate for 1 hour to marinate. Thread the prawns onto skewers and heat a griddle pan over a high heat. Brush the prawns with a little olive oil and cook in batches, for 3–4 minutes, or until cooked through.

Serve the char-grilled prawns with the romesco sauce, roasted onions, griddled sourdough and salad leaves.

PAN-FRIED COD FILLET
with white polenta & basil gremolata

This cod fillet is pan-fried until the skin crisps up, and then a light lemon butter is sizzled in the same pan, ready to spoon over to serve. White polenta is given an umami-flavour boost with Parmesan, and the whole dish is finished off with the fresh zing of a green herb and garlic gremolata.

2 teaspoons olive oil
4 x 200-g/8-oz. cod fillets, skin on
40 g/3 tablespoons butter
freshly squeezed juice of 1 lemon
a large handful of fresh basil,
   leaves picked
sea salt and black pepper
samphire, to serve (optional)

WHITE POLENTA
1½ litres/6 cups vegetable stock
250 ml/1 cup milk
350 g/2 cups white polenta/
   cornmeal
3 tablespoons finely grated
   Parmesan
50 g/3½ tablespoons butter,
   coarsely chopped

BASIL GREMOLATA
finely grated zest and juice
   of 1 lemon
3 tablespoons olive oil
2 garlic cloves, crushed
½ a bunch of fresh flat-leaf
   parsley, finely chopped
½ a bunch of fresh basil,
   finely chopped

SERVES 4

For the polenta, bring the vegetable stock and milk to a simmer in a saucepan over a medium heat. Add the polenta in a thin steady stream, whisk continuously until all is incorporated, then stir occasionally for about 15–20 minutes until the polenta is cooked through. Stir through the Parmesan and butter. Keep warm while you cook the cod.

For the gremolata, mix together the lemon zest and juice, olive oil, garlic, parsley and basil in a bowl and set aside.

Lightly coat the base of a non-stick frying pan/skillet with olive oil, then place the pan over a medium-high heat. Once the pan is hot, season the cod pieces with salt, then place them in the pan, skin-side down. Cook for 2–3 minutes until the skin is nicely golden and crisp. Carefully turn the cod over and cook for a further 2–3 minutes, depending on the thickness of the fillet or loin. The fish is cooked when the flesh becomes opaque. Add the butter, squeeze over the lemon juice, season with salt and let it bubble and brown.

Serve the cooked cod on warmed plates with the polenta, topped with the gremolata and basil leaves and spoonfuls of the lemon butter and samphire on the side, if liked. I enjoy this with a cold glass of rosé wine.

SMOKED TARAMASALATA,
with asparagus & crisp pitta

Forget the bright pink shop-bought version – after making this taramasalata yourself, you will never go back! Served alongside your own pitta crisps and griddled vegetables, this makes either an impressive first course or a side for a seafood extravaganza.

SMOKED TARAMASALATA

150 g/5½ oz. smoked cod roe,
 skin removed
4 thick sourdough bread slices,
 crusts removed, coarsely torn
½ small onion, grated
1 garlic clove, crushed
160 ml/generous ⅔ cup olive oil
freshly squeezed juice of
 1½ lemons
black pepper
salmon roe and fresh oregano,
 to serve

CRISP PITTA

4 large pitta or other flat bread
 (see pages 170 and 174),
 or store bought
80 ml/⅓ cup extra virgin olive oil
1 teaspoon sesame seeds
1 teaspoon dried oregano

ASPARAGUS

bunch of asparagus, trimmed
2 tablespoons olive oil
3 spring onions/scallions,
 finely sliced
200 g/7 oz. radishes
freshly squeezed juice of ½ lemon

SERVES 4–6 TO SHARE

For the smoked taramasalata, place the cod roe in a non-reactive bowl, cover with water and soak for 30 minutes to remove the salt, then drain. Place the bread in a separate bowl, cover with water, soak for 15 minutes until softened, then drain and gently squeeze out any excess water. Process the roe, bread, onion and garlic in a food processor to combine. With the motor running, add the oil in a thin steady stream and blend until thick and emulsified. Season with black pepper and the lemon juice and refrigerate until required. It will keep refrigerated in an airtight container for up to 1 week.

Meanwhile, for crisp pitta bread, preheat the oven to 200°C fan/220°C/450°F/gas 7. Cut the bread into small triangles and place in a single layer on baking sheets lined with baking paper. Drizzle with olive oil, scatter with sesame seeds and oregano, turn and repeat. Bake in the preheated oven for 15 minutes turning once, until golden and crisp, then leave to cool to room temperature.

Meanwhile, cook the asparagus in a large saucepan of boiling salted water for 2–3 minutes until just tender, then drain. Preheat a griddle pan, brush the spring onions and radishes with oil and char-grill for a few minutes until softened (if you wish, the cooked asparagus can also be popped into the pan).

Spoon the taramasalata into a bowl and top with salmon roe and oregano and put the crisp pitta in another bowl. Place the asparagus, spring onions and radishes on a serving plate and squeeze over the lemon juice.

CLASSIC BOUILLABAISSE *with basil rouille*

Bouillabaisse is a traditional Provençal fish stew originating in the port city of Marseille. This classic French dish makes the most of the freshest of seafood arriving by boat and is lovely simply served with some bread and the basil rouille.

500 g/1 lb. 2 oz. tomatoes
1 tablespoon olive oil
2 onions, finely chopped
5 garlic cloves, 4 crushed and
    1 cut in half
2 sprigs each fresh thyme,
    oregano and basil
1 fresh bay leaf
8 tiger prawns/jumbo shrimp,
    heads removed, tails intact,
    shells reserved
pinch of saffron threads
20 ml/¾ fl. oz. Pernod
2 strips of orange peel
8 thick sourdough bread slices
1 kg/2¼ lb. filleted mixed
    Mediterranean fish, each fillet
    cut into large chunks
200 g/7 oz. mussels (optional)
sea salt and black pepper
fresh parsley, to garnish

BASIL ROUILLE
1 egg yolk
1 garlic clove, finely chopped
1 teaspoon Dijon mustard
1 teaspoon tomato purée/paste
200 ml/¾–1 cup olive oil
20 g/¾ oz. fresh basil leaves

SERVES 4

Blanch the tomatoes in a large saucepan of boiling water for 30 seconds until the skins split, then refresh in cold water, peel, remove and discard seeds, coarsely chop the flesh and set aside.

Heat half the olive oil in a large saucepan over a medium heat, add the onions, crushed garlic and herbs and sauté for 5–7 minutes until the onions soften. Increase the heat to high, add the prawn shells and saffron and stir occasionally for 5–7 minutes until pink. Add the tomatoes and 1 litre/quart water and simmer gently for 25–30 minutes until infused. Strain through a fine sieve into a clean saucepan, pressing on the solids to extract all the liquid and flavour. Discard the solids. Add the Pernod and the orange peel, season to taste and keep the stock warm.

Meanwhile, make the rouille. Put the egg yolk, garlic, mustard and tomato purée in a food processor and blend until well combined. With the motor running, add the oil in a thin steady stream until incorporated and the rouille is thick. Add the basil and blitz until the mixture is green and smooth. Season to taste, set aside until required.

Preheat a chargrill pan over high heat. Drizzle the bread with the remaining olive oil, season to taste and grill/broil, turning once, for 1–2 minutes per side until golden. Rub with the cut-side of the garlic, set aside and keep warm.

Bring the strained stock to a low simmer, add the fish and mussels and simmer for 10 minutes. Season to taste and serve hot, scattered with parsley, with a dollop of rouille and the grilled sourdough.

DEEP-FRIED SQUID & POTATOES
with garlic mayonnaise

This is inspired by the catch of the day on the Mediterranean coast. Here the freshest of squid are fried with potatoes and served with garlic mayonnaise and a glass of cold beer.

4 Desiree potatoes, skin on, cut into 3-cm/1¼-in. pieces
400 ml/1¾ cups olive oil
10 fresh flat-leaf parsley sprigs
300 g/10½ oz. squid (about 6), cleaned, cut into 2-cm/¾-in. pieces
plain/all-purpose flour, seasoned with a few pinches of cayenne pepper, for dusting
sea salt and black pepper
lemon wedges, to serve

GARLIC MAYONNAISE
2 garlic cloves, peeled
100 g/3½ oz. Mayonnaise (see page 158) or shop-bought
½ teaspoon Dijon mustard
pinch of cayenne pepper
1–2 teaspoons freshly squeezed lemon juice

SERVES 4 TO SHARE

Cook the potatoes and garlic (for the mayonnaise) in boiling salted water until tender for about 15 minutes. Drain and spread on a baking sheet to steam and cool.

Mash the garlic and add to a bowl with the other garlic mayonnaise ingredients and set aside.

Heat the oil in a deep frying pan/skillet over a medium-high heat, add potatoes in batches and fry, turning occasionally, until golden. Remove with a slotted spoon and set aside on paper towels and keep warm. Add the parsley sprigs in batches and cook for 30 seconds until crispy, being careful not to burn. Remove with a slotted spoon.

Dust the squid in the seasoned flour, shaking off any excess. Fry in batches in the same pan as the potatoes for 2–3 minutes until golden, then drain on paper towels.

Scatter the potatoes, squid and parsley on a serving platter. Season to taste and serve with lemon wedges and the garlic mayonnaise.

BRAISED BEANS, CHORIZO & CALAMARI

This is a winning dish that brings classic flavours and simple comforts together in a single bowl. Served alongside the Deep-fried Squid and Potatoes (see page 40) and some chunky bread, it makes for a lovely seafood lunch. Alternatively, it's great just eaten in a bowl on its own.

2 tablespoons extra virgin olive oil
1 chorizo ring, chopped into
    chunks
1 garlic clove, crushed
1 teaspoon smoked paprika
500 g/1 lb. 2 oz. squid, cleaned
    and cut into rounds
200 g/7 oz. cherry tomatoes,
    halved
20 ml/4 teaspoons sherry
200 ml/¾–1 cup vegetable stock
400-g/14-oz. can cannellini beans,
    drained
1 tablespoon fresh majoram leaves
1 tablespoon fresh thyme leaves

SERVES 4 TO SHARE

Heat the oil in a large frying pan/skillet over a high heat, add the chorizo, garlic and paprika and cook until the chorizo is crisp and the oil is coloured red. Remove the chorizo with a slotted spoon and set aside.

Return the pan to a high heat, add the squid and cook at a high temperature, stirring occasionally, for 4–5 minutes until it turns opaque and is just cooked through. Add the cherry tomatoes to the pan. Add the sherry and stir for 4–5 minutes until reduced. Add the vegetable stock and beans and return the chorizo to the pan. Cook, stirring, for about 8–10 minutes until combined.

Transfer to a platter, scatter with herbs and serve immediately.

ALL-IN-ONE SALMON *with potatoes, tomatoes & artichokes with green olive tapenade*

This is one of those fantastic all-rounders. It's great as a family meal, entertaining friends, casual dinner or made in advance and turned into a salad the next day. All the ingredients are very simple, but when they come together they make something very special.

2 red onions, sliced

400 g/14 oz. potatoes, scrubbed and thickly sliced

3 tablespoons olive oil

1 tablespoon dried oregano

250 g/9 oz. tomatoes, halved

4 garlic cloves, roughly chopped

2 fresh rosemary sprigs, leaves picked and chopped

2 red (bell) peppers, thickly sliced

4 salmon fillets, skin on

100 g/3½ oz. marinated artichokes

4 bay leaves

sea salt and black pepper

1 lemon

flat-leaf parsley, to garnish

red onion, to garnish

30 g/2 tablespoons Green Olive Tapenade (see page 165), to serve

Quick Pickled Cucumber (see page 153), to serve

SERVES 4

Preheat the oven to 180°C fan/200°C/400°F/gas 6.

Put the potatoes and onions in a large baking dish and toss with 1 tablespoon of the oil and the oregano. Bake in the preheated oven for 15 minutes.

Stir in the tomatoes, garlic, rosemary and red peppers and another 1 teaspoon of the oil. Top with the salmon fillets, drizzle each fillet with a little oil and season. Add the artichokes and bay leaves. Cover the dish with foil and bake for 8–10 minutes or until the fish is cooked through and the potatoes are browned and crisp.

Remove the baking dish from the oven. Squeeze the lemon over the fish and scatter with the parsley and red onion. Serve with the tapenade and cucumber pickle.

salt

Salt has been used by humans for thousands of years, for seasoning and food preservation. In fact it's due to the art of preserving food that civilization developed, helping prolong food when out of season and enabling transportation of food over large distances. There is evidence that salt has been used as part of Ancient Egyptian offerings and in valuable trade between the Phoenecians and their Mediterranean Empire. The word 'salary' was derived from the word 'salt' – as salt was so valuable, soldiers in the Roman army were sometimes paid with salt instead of money. Their monthly allowance was called 'salarium' ('sal' being the Latin word for salt).

Salt is so much more than a granular seasoning in a shaker. It is an essential element in the diet of humans, animals and plants.

When looking at salt the texture and shape are very important : The texture refers to the shape of the individual granules of salt. They can be cubic, star-like or as irregular as snowflakes. If salt has a chunky, large and irregular shape, you probably should be using it as a finishing salt. Understanding salinity (basically how salty it is) is important, for example, table salt is saltier than sea salt. Have a little taste before using it.

Types of salt

IODISED SALT/TABLE SALT Everybody knows this salt, as it is found in salt shakers the world over. It is also called iodized salt because it contains potassium iodide. The taste is more metallic due to an anti-caking agent and potassium iodide. It is best used for general cooking purposes.

ROCK OR KOSHER SALT This has a perfect middle-of-the-road texture that is easily dissolvable, so always taste your dishes as you cook. It is best used for general cooking purposes.

SEA SALT This is salt which uses the ocean's salinity. On a very basic level, sea water is boiled down until all that's left is the salt. It can come in a number of different textures and salinities. This is best used for finishing or general cooking needs, depending on texture.

FLAKY SALT The name is determined by the texture. If the individual pieces of salt are big but not uniform in size, and have a flat-ish shape, then you have flaky salt. If you look closely, the shape is like a snowflake, and all the flakes are different, too. It is best used as a finishing salt.

FLEUR DE SEL Fleur de sel are the crystal formed naturally on the surface of salt evaporation ponds, and collected using wooden tools. The collection only takes place once a year in the summer when the weather is perfect. It is best used as a finishing salt.

HIMALAYAN PINK SALT This salt comes from the Himalayan Mountains of Pakistan, but is very readily available and used throughout the world. It gets its iconic colour from natural minerals that vary from deep reds to light pinks. The uses are versatile; you can use it in salads, on meat, on vegetables, or even to garnish the rim of a cocktail glass.

SMOKED OR FLAVOURED SALT Infusing different flavours into salt is a great way to add some variety to a dish. The smokey flavour of smoked salt is perfect for hardier dishes, while gentler herb-infused salts suit more delicate ones. Other flavoured salts use the addition of herbs or spices, such as rosemary salt, truffle salt or chipotle salt, while tastes can get even fancier with black garlic salt or wine salt.

FOR THE TABLE: A SUMMER SEAFOOD BBQ

All these recipes stand alone beautifully, but when all placed together
they create a summer seafood bbq feast. From blackened salmon, grilled
sardines and squid salad to a delicious fish burger with tartare sauce.
Perfect served in the warm sunshine, with free-flowing chilled white wine.
Pictured on pages 50–51

BLACKENED SALMON WITH LETTUCE, WATERCRESS & *yogurt sauce*

*Spicy, charred salmon cooled down with a yogurt sauce on a bed of
lettuce and watercress – perfect for a sharing table with a selection
of other dishes or serve with Pan-fried Baby Potatoes with Garlic,
Sage and Olives (see page 105) for a complete meal on its own.*

1 tablespoon smoked paprika
1 teaspoon dried oregano
1 tablespoon brown sugar
1 garlic clove, crushed
2–3 tablespoons olive oil
4 skinless salmon fillets
100 g/3½ oz. watercress, to serve
sea salt and black pepper

YOGURT SAUCE
150 g/5½ oz. Greek yogurt
grated zest and juice of 1 lemon
1 teaspoon honey
½ bunch fresh parsley, finely
   chopped

SERVES 4–6 TO SHARE

Preheat a barbecue grill.

In a bowl, mix the paprika, oregano, sugar, garlic and olive oil to make
a paste. Brush the paste over the salmon fillets and season well with
salt and pepper.

Place the fish onto a hot barbecue skin side-down and cook for
2 minutes. Then turn over and cook for 3–4 minutes until the salmon
is cooked through and just 'blackened' by the spices.

If cooking under a grill/broiler, preheat to high and line a baking sheet
with non-stick baking paper. Put the fish on the lined baking sheet
and give an extra drizzle of olive oil. Grill/broil for 6–8 minutes, until
cooked through.

Make the yogurt sauce by mixing the yogurt, lemon zest and juice,
honey, parsley and salt and pepper in a bowl and set aside until needed.

Serve the blackened salmon with the yogurt sauce and the watercress.

FISH BURGERS *with tartare sauce*

This great summer fish burger is light and will become your barbecue staple. Elevate it to even greater heights by serving with a tangy tartare sauce, tomatoes, onions and lettuce on a soft seeded bun.

FISH BURGERS

400 g/14 oz. white fish fillet, boneless and skinless

300 g/10½ oz. salmon fillet, boneless and skinless

2 garlic cloves, crushed

2 tablespoons capers, drained and chopped

1 tablespoon fresh dill, chopped

1 tablespoon wholegrain mustard

1 tablespoon fresh parsley, chopped

3 spring onions/scallions, finely chopped

grated zest of 1 lemon (reserve the juice)

1 teaspoon bicarbonate of soda/ baking soda

4 white buns or brioche buns

1 beef tomato, sliced

1 onion, thinly sliced

1 Little Gem lettuce, leaves separated

sea salt and black pepper

TARTARE SAUCE

150 g/5½ oz. mayonnaise (store bought or see page 158)

2 shallots, finely chopped

40 g/1½ oz. cornichons, finely chopped

2 tablespoons salted capers, well-rinsed and chopped

½ bunch fresh flat-leaf parsley, coarsely chopped

SERVES 4

Place the fish fillets on a plate. Sprinkle over 1 tablespoon of sea salt, cover, then place the fish in the fridge for 1½–2 hours.

Rinse the fish thoroughly under running cold water, then drain well on paper towels and pat dry. Finely chop all the fish with a sharp knife and transfer to a bowl. Add the garlic, capers, dill, mustard, parsley, spring onions, lemon zest and bicarbonate of soda (it helps to firm up the burgers) and mix together. Shape into 4 large burgers, cover with clingfilm/plastic wrap and chill for at least 1 hour before cooking.

Meanwhile, make the tartare sauce by mixing all the ingredients together in a bowl and set aside until needed.

When ready to cook, preheat the barbecue.

Slice the buns, then toast the cut sides and set aside.

Add the fish burgers to the hot grill and cook for 5–7 minutes on each side until cooked through and lightly coloured. Remove to a warm dish and cover with foil to keep hot. Divide the tomato slices between the buns and then add the fish burgers, onion and lettuce and a good dollop of tartare sauce.

PROVENÇAL SQUID SALAD
with tarragon & fresh mint

A juicy colourful summer salad that works well as the main event for
a light lunch or as a salad for barbecue lunch. Very versatile, and great
served with a chilled glass of crisp white wine.

30 ml/2 tablespoons olive oil

2 garlic cloves, sliced

pinch of chilli/hot red pepper flakes

500 g/1 lb. 2 oz. squid, cleaned
(ask your fishmonger to do this
for you) and scored

grated zest and juice of 1 lemon

200 g/7 oz. cherry tomatoes,
quartered

1 tablespoon capers

200 g/7 oz. green beans, blanched
and refreshed in cold water

2 fresh tarragon sprigs, leaves
picked

3 fresh mint sprigs, leaves picked

1 tablespoon toasted almonds,
chopped

sea salt and black pepper

crusty baguette, to serve

SERVES 4 TO SHARE

Gently heat the oil in a large frying pan/skillet over a medium heat. Add the sliced garlic and sauté gently, not to add colour, just to gently cook. Add the chilli flakes and some salt and pepper and sauté for about 3 minutes.

Raise the heat to high, add the squid to the pan and season again. Cook for a few minutes until just firm and opaque. Add the lemon zest and juice, tomatoes and capers and cook for a few more minutes, then take off the heat and leave to cool.

Once the mixture has cooled, place in a bowl and add all the remaining ingredients. Serve with a crusty baguette on the side. This can be eaten, just warm, at room temperature or chilled with a lovely glass of wine.

GRILLED SARDINES *with piquillo peppers,*
Puy lentils & pickled onions

This recipe is best made with the freshest of in-season sardines. Nothing evokes a sense of the Mediterranean more than the aroma of sardines grilling. Here the fish sit on a bed of lentils and piquillo peppers and are finished off with pickled onions, to pair with the oiliness of the fish.

grated zest and freshly squeezed
   juice of 1 lemon, plus 2 lemons,
   halved
1 red chilli/chile, deseeded and
   finely chopped
1 garlic clove, crushed
2 tablespoons olive oil
8 x 100 g/3½ oz. sardines, gutted

PIQUILLO LENTIL BASE
4 tablespoons olive oil
1 small onion, peeled and cut into
   eighths
1 carrot, diced
1 small leek, sliced into thin rings
2 garlic cloves, chopped
200 g/generous 1 cup cooked
   Puy lentils
200 ml/¾ cup fish or vegetable
   stock
1 bay leaf
100 g/3½ oz. piquillo peppers,
   cut into strips
1 red onion, finely sliced
3 tablespoons Forum cabernet
   sauvignon vinegar
handful of fresh herbs
   (parsley, chervil and mint)
sea salt and black pepper

TO SERVE
pickled onions, crusty bread
   and salad leaves

SERVES 4

First, make the lentil base. Heat 2 tablespoons olive oil in a heavy-based pan, then fry the onion, carrot, leek and garlic for 5 minutes until they just start to soften. Add the lentils and coat with the oil. Cover the lentils with the stock, add the bay leaf and cook until thickened. Finish with the remaining olive oil and fresh herbs, then set aside.

In a small bowl, mix together the lemon zest and 2 teaspoons lemon juice with the chilli, garlic and oil. Season with salt and black pepper.

Make small slits on one side of each sardine. Rub the lemon and oil mixture all over the sardines, rubbing well into the slits and body cavity.

Cook the sardines on a hot barbecue grill (or over a medium-high heat in a griddle pan) for 3 minutes on each side until cooked through and the flesh flakes away easily from the bone.

Put the lemon halves, cut-side-down, next to the fish for the final 3 minutes of the cooking time.

To serve. spread the lentil mixture over a serving platter, add the salad leaves and top with the sardines. Scatter over the pickled onions and serve with bread.

LOBSTER & CHERRY TOMATO LINGUINE
from Santorini

Imagine being seated at a wooden table in a little restaurant in the town of Oia in Santorini, with a view of the caldera and a platter of this lobster linguine in front of you. The sauce is infused with a touch of cinnamon and white wine, and is perfect with the succulent lobster tails.

4 lobster tails, uncooked
400 ml/1¾ cups fish stock
2 bay leaves
200 g/7 oz. linguine
60 g/4 tablespoons butter, divided
1 onion, finely chopped
2 garlic cloves
200 g/7 oz. cherry tomatoes
2 tablespoons tomato purée/paste
1 teaspoon honey
pinch of chilli/hot red pepper flakes
100 ml/⅓ cup plus 1 tablespoon
    white wine
1 teaspoon smoked paprika
2 cloves
½ teaspoon ground cinnamon
sea salt and black pepper

SERVES 2

Place the lobster tails in a large pot with the fish stock and bay leaves. Bring to the boil, then reduce to a medium heat and steam for 7–8 minutes. Remove the lobsters, reserving the cooking liquid.

In the same pot you cooked the lobsters in, season the reserved cooking liquid with salt and add the linguine. Cook until just under al dente. Drain, but do not rinse, reserving at least 300 ml/1½ cups of cooking liquid.

Meanwhile, melt 1 tablespoon of the butter in a large sauté pan over a medium heat. Add the onion and garlic and cook for about 3 minutes until softened. Season with salt. Add the cherry tomatoes, tomato purée, honey and chilli flakes and cook for 1 minute. Add the wine and cook for about 2 minutes until reduced by half. Add the reserved lobster cooking liquid, paprika, cloves and cinnamon and simmer for 2–3 minutes. Stir in the remaining butter.

Add the lobster tails to the sauce, stirring to cover them well with sauce. Add the linguine along with about 60 ml/¼ cup of the reserved pasta cooking liquid and toss to coat in the sauce (the heat should still be on medium). Add more reserved pasta cooking liquid if needed. Cook until the sauce has thickened and the pasta is al dente. Season to taste with salt and pepper.

Place the linguine and tomatoes on a big serving platter and top with the lobster pieces.

CHARRED TUNA NIÇOISE
with Dijon & anchovy dressing

As in the name, this is inspired by the salad that originates from Nice in southern France. There are many heated debates on what constitutes a 'true' Niçoise salad and there are variations. This one uses tuna steak that is charred and is quite a substantial main course.

200 g/7 oz. baby green beans, trimmed and cut into 3-cm/1¼-in. lengths

2 eggs, at room temperature

300 g/10½ oz. tuna fillet

150 g/5½ oz. mini new potatoes, boiled and cooled

150 g/5½ oz. cherry tomatoes, quartered

50 g/1¾ oz. small black olives, stoned/pitted

2 shallots, thinly shaved on a mandolin

½ bunch of small fresh basil leaves, coarsely torn

200 g/7 oz. baby spinach leaves

sea salt and black pepper

oil, for brushing

baguette slices, to serve

ANCHOVY DRESSING

60 ml/¼ cup extra virgin olive oil

1 tablespoon freshly squeezed lemon juice

1 tablespoon red wine vinegar

1 teaspoon Dijon mustard

3 anchovy fillets, finely chopped

1 garlic clove, crushed

SERVES 2

To make the dressing, whisk the oil, lemon juice, vinegar, mustard, anchovy and garlic in a bowl together and season to taste with black pepper. Set aside until needed. (This makes double the quantity needed, so the remainder can be stored in the fridge for a few days.)

Preheat a griddle pan or barbecue.

Blanch the beans in a saucepan of boiling salted water over a medium-high heat for 1–2 minutes until just tender. Drain, refresh in cold water, drain well and transfer to a bowl.

Add the eggs to a pan of boiling water and cook for 6 minutes for soft yolks. Drain, refresh under cold running water, peel and cut in half.

Season the tuna steak, brush with oil on each side and cook on the hot griddle pan or barbecue for 2–3 minutes on each side. Remove and slice.

Divide the charred tuna, beans, new potatoes, cherry tomatoes, olives, shallots, basil and spinach between two plates and toss to combine. Season to taste and drizzle with the dressing to serve.

de terra

FROM THE LAND
Meat

STEAK & CHIPS *with deep wine jus*

The labour of love in this dish is the deep wine jus, but it can be made in advance and refrigerated. This is best served on a sharing plater for two, for you to share and savour every last morsel.

4 large Maris Piper potatoes, peeled and cut into chunky strips
vegetable oil, for deep frying and drizzling
700 g/1½ lb. T-bone steak
2 garlic cloves, bashed
½ small pack of fresh thyme
1 tablespoon olive oil
50 g/3½ tablespoons butter
watercress, to serve

DEEP WINE JUS STOCK
1 chicken carcass, reserved from roasting chicken
3 carrots, coarsely chopped
3 celery stalks, coarsely chopped
1 onion, peeled and cut in half
1 head of garlic, halved widthways
1 teaspoon black peppercorns
1 bouquet garni (4 bay leaves, ½ bunch thyme, handful of parsley on stems, tied together with string)

WINE REDUCTION
2 large golden shallots, thinly sliced
½ bunch fresh thyme
2 bay leaves
½ teaspoon black peppercorns
500 ml/generous 2 cups red wine
1 garlic clove, thinly sliced

SERVES 2 TO SHARE

To make the stock, preheat the oven to 160°C fan/180°C/350°F/gas 4. Place the chicken carcass and vegetables in a large roasting pan and roast for 30 minutes until golden. Transfer the carcass and vegetables to a stock pot, add peppercorns, bouquet garni and enough water to cover. Bring to the boil over a high heat, then simmer over a very low heat for 2–3 hours, occasionally skimming any scum from surface. Strain through a muslin-lined fine sieve. Cool, then refrigerate for 2–3 hours until the fat has separated from the stock. Skim the fat from the top and discard.

For the wine reduction, combine all ingredients in a pan, bring to the boil over a high heat, reduce heat to medium-high and cook for 20 minutes until reduced to about 180 ml/¾ cup. Strain. Add the stock to the pan. Bring to the boil over a high heat, reduce to medium and cook, skimming frequently, for 1¼ hours until reduced to 480 ml/2 cups. The jus will keep in the fridge for up to 1 week or can be frozen in batches.

For the chips, wash the potatoes well in cold water and pat dry with a clean tea/dish towel. Fill a deep-fat fryer or a large, deep, heavy-bottomed saucepan two-thirds full with vegetable oil. Heat the oil to 180°C/350°F. Deep-fry the chips in batches for 2 minutes until crisp and golden brown. Drain on paper towels and season lightly with salt.

Preheat the oven to 180°C fan/200°C/400°F/gas 6. Set an ovenproof griddle pan over a high heat. Season the steak on both sides, then rub both sides with the garlic cloves, thyme and olive oil. Put the steak in the hot pan and char the underside for 2 minutes until griddle lines appear. Turn over to brown the other side, rub the top with the thyme again, then lay the thyme and garlic on top of the meat. Once evenly browned with griddle lines, put the thyme and garlic to one side. Hold the steak with tongs to cook its fatty side for a few minutes and render it down so it's soft rather than gristly. Lay the steak flat again, put the thyme, garlic and the butter on top and transfer the pan to the oven for 4-5 minutes until the meat reaches 62–65°C/144–149°F on a probe thermometer (or until cooked to your liking). Rest the meat for 5–6 minutes. Serve on a board or large plate in the middle of the table, with the chips, jus and watercress.

LAMB CUTLETS WITH HARISSA & HONEY *with*
green tomatoes, shaved cucumber & giant couscous

Lamb cutlets are the Rolls Royce of lamb cuts, but are they worth it. Gently spiced with harissa and honey and served on a bed giant couscous, chopped green tomatoes, ribbons of cucumber and some pickled grapes. A perfect alternative for Sunday lunch alfresco.

200 g/1 cup Greek yogurt
1 heaped tablespoon harissa
1 heaped tablespoon honey
4 lamb cutlets, 180–200 g/6–7 oz.
    each
sea salt and black pepper

COUSCOUS
100 g/3½ oz. giant couscous
125 ml/½ cup hot vegetable stock
400-g/14-oz. can chickpeas,
    drained
grated zest and juice of 1 lemon
1 tablespoon white wine vinegar
6 dried apricots, chopped
30 g/1 oz. fresh mint
30 g/1 oz. Bay and Juniper-Pickled
    Grapes (see page 156)

**TOMATOES WITH SHAVED
CUCUMBER**
200 g/7oz. green and orange
    tomatoes (or red ones),
    roughly chopped
2 small cucumbers, sliced into
    ribbons
freshly squeezed juice of 1 lemon
1 tablespoon olive oil

SERVES 2

Heat the grill/broiler.

In a large bowl, mix the yogurt and half the harissa with some seasoning. Remove 2 tablespoons, set aside, then add the lamb to the remainder and leave to marinate while you make the couscous (or leave in the fridge overnight, if you prefer).

In a bowl mix the chopped tomatoes and sliced cucumber with the lemon juice and olive oil. Season well, then set aside.

In a bowl, cover the couscous with the hot stock and add the remaining harissa. Cover with clingfilm/plastic wrap and leave for 5 minutes, then stir in the chickpeas, lemon zest and juice, vinegar, apricots and half the mint.

Transfer the lamb cutlets to a baking sheet and grill/broil for 2–3 minutes each side, pouring any cooking juices into the couscous for extra flavour.

Serve the lamb with the couscous, pickled grapes, tomatoes and cucumber, reserved yogurt and a scattering of mint.

BEEF MOUSSAKA *with yogurt béchamel*

In Greek households this is a special occasion recipe as it takes a long time to make, but the result is a beautiful depth of flavour. Traditionally the potatoes and aubergines would be fried, but baking them brings a lightness to the dish, as does the yogurt béchamel.

2½ tablespoons olive oil

1 onion, chopped

2 garlic cloves, finely chopped

2 large carrots (350 g/12½ oz. total weight), diced

450 g/1 lb. 5% fat minced/ground beef

100 ml/generous ⅓ cup white wine

1 teaspoon ground cinnamon, plus extra for spinkling

¼ teaspoon ground allspice

400-g/14-oz. can plum tomatoes

2 tablespoons tomato purée/paste

1 heaped tablespoon chopped fresh oregano leaves

2 good handfuls of chopped fresh flat-leaf parsley, plus extra to garnish

3 aubergines/eggplants (about 750 g/1 lb. 10 oz. total weight), ends trimmed

3 large potatoes, peeled and sliced

freshly squeezed juice of 1 lemon

sea salt and black pepper

TOPPING

2 eggs

1 tablespoon cornflour/cornstarch

300 g/10½ oz. 2% fat Greek yogurt

50 g/⅔ cup grated Parmesan

3–4 bay leaves

28 x 20 x 6-cm/11 x 8 x 2½-in. ovenproof dish

SERVES 6

Heat 1 tablespoon of the oil in a large, wide sauté pan. Add the onion and garlic and fry for 6–8 minutes until turning golden. Add the carrots and fry for 2 minutes. Stir the meat into the pan, breaking it up as you stir. Cook and stir over a high heat until the meat is no longer pink. Pour in the wine and briefly cook until most of the liquid has evaporated. Stir in the cinnamon and allspice. Tip in the tomatoes, tomato purée and 1 tablespoon water (mixed with any juices left in the can), then stir to break up the tomatoes. Season with some pepper, add all the oregano and half the parsley, cover, then simmer over a low heat for 50 minutes, stirring occasionally. Season to taste and mix in the remaining parsley. This can be done a day ahead and refrigerated overnight.

Meanwhile, prepare the aubergines. Preheat the oven to 180°C fan/200°C/400°F/gas 6. Brush a little of the remaining oil onto 2 large baking sheets. Mix the rest of the oil with the lemon juice. Slice the aubergines into 1-cm/½-in. lengthways slices, then lay them on the oiled baking sheets along with the sliced potatoes. Brush with the oil and lemon mix, then season with pepper. Bake for 20–25 minutes until soft, then set aside. Lower the oven temperature to 160°C fan/180°C/350°F/gas 4.

Spread 2 big spoonfuls of the meat mixture on the bottom of an ovenproof dish. Lay the aubergine and potato slices on top, slightly overlapping. Spoon the rest of the meat mixture on top.

To make the topping, beat the eggs in a bowl. Slacken the cornflour with a little of the yogurt, stir in the rest of the yogurt, then mix this into the eggs with half the cheese. Season with pepper. Pour and spread this over the meat to cover it. Sprinkle with the rest of the cheese, a little cinnamon and a grating of pepper, and top with the bay leaves. Bake for 50–60 minutes until bubbling and golden. Leave the moussaka to settle for 8–10 minutes, then cut into squares to serve.

POACHED CHICKEN BREASTS
with wild garlic salsa verde & radishes

*Gently poaching the chicken and serving it with the wild garlic salsa
and thinly sliced radishes results in a delicate dish for a summer meal.
If the wild garlic is out of season, you can use a selection of soft green
herbs instead. This dish tastes clean and fresh.*

SALSA VERDE

20 g/¾ oz. wild garlic or 2 garlic
 cloves, crushed

3 anchovy fillets, finely chopped

15 g/½ oz. fresh flat-leaf parsley,
 coarsely chopped

2 tablespoons small capers in
 vinegar, rinsed and drained

1 tablespoon white wine vinegar

grated zest and juice of ½ lemon

80 ml/⅓ cup extra virgin olive oil

sea salt and black pepper

POACHED CHICKEN

1 carrot, roughly sliced

1 celery stick, roughly chopped

3 large garlic cloves

½ small bunch of fresh parsley

3 lemon rinds

4 skinless boneless chicken breasts

TO SERVE

blanched fresh broad/fava beans,
 watercress and radishes

SERVES 4

For the salsa verde, blend the garlic leaves or garlic cloves, anchovies, parsley, capers, vinegar and lemon zest and juice to a coarse paste in a food processor. With the motor running, add the olive oil in a thin steady stream, then season to taste. Set aside until ready to use.

For the poached chicken, put the carrot, celery and garlic in a large saucepan. Add the parsley, lemon rinds, salt, chicken breasts, and 1 litre/4 cups cold water (adding a little more water if it doesn't quite cover the chicken). Bring to the boil, then immediately lower to a simmer and cook over a very low heat for 10–12 minutes, or until the juices run clear in the thickest part of the breast.

Remove the pan from the heat and scoop out the chicken breasts from the poaching liquid. Slice or tear the chicken, serve with the broad beans, watercress, radishes and a drizzle of salsa verde.

BAKED CANNELLONI

A family favourite always. Make double and freeze one uncooked, ready to go for when you have not had enough time to cook from scratch. It also makes the perfect gift for someone – giving food is giving life.

BECHAMEL

120 g/½ cup unsalted butter, plus extra for greasing

90 g/⅔ cup plain/all-purpose flour

½ small nutmeg, finely grated

1 litre/4 cups whole milk

50 g/⅔ cup grated Parmessan

1 ball of mozzrella, torn

sea salt and black pepper

BEEF, RICOTTA & SPINACH FILLING

60 ml/¼ cup extra virgin olive oil

1 onion, finely chopped

300 g/10½ oz.minced/ground beef

1 tablespoon sundried tomato paste

250 g/9 oz. ricotta

½ nutmeg, finely grated

300 g/10½ oz. spinach, coarsely chopped

100 g/1⅓ cups grated Parmesan

20 g/¾ oz. mixed fresh herbs (parsley, thyme and basil), chopped

5 fresh lasagne sheets, cut into 15 x 12-cm/6 x 4¾-in. rectangles

20 x 30-cm/8 x 12-in. ovenproof baking dish

SERVES 4–6

Preheat the oven to 160°C fan/180°C/350°F/gas 4. Grease the ovenproof baking dish.

For the béchamel, combine the butter, flour and nutmeg in a saucepan. Whisk until the mixture begins to brown. Gradually add the milk, whisking constantly until smooth, then bring the mixture to a simmer. Remove from the heat, season to taste and continue stirring for a few minutes until thickened. Set aside.

For the beef filling, heat the oil in a large saucepan over a low heat. Add the onion and stir occasionally until translucent. Add the beef, season to taste and cook, stirring occasionally, until browned, then add the sundried tomato paste. Cool, then add the ricotta, nutmeg, and 2 tablespoons of the béchamel, stirring to combine. Fold in the spinach, Parmesan and mixed herbs.

Lay a lasagne sheet on a flat surface, top with 2 tablespoons of the beef and ricotta filling along the centre and roll the lasagne sheet up to enclose it. Place in the baking dish, seam-side down, then repeat with the remaining sheets and filling.

Cover evenly with any remaining beef and ricotta sauce, the remaining béchamel and then sprinkle with Parmesan and mozzarella. Bake in the preheated oven for about 30 minutes until the cheese is melted and the edges are golden.

PORK SKEWERS ON YOGURT FLATBREAD & HOMEMADE SWEET POTATO CHIPS *with crispy salad & lemon & oregano yogurt dressing*

My father Theo Kordalis always marinates souvlaki in lager overnight, which tenderizes and deeply flavours the meat, resulting in succulent souvlaki. He cuts the pork tenderloin a little larger and threads the skewers with sage. The best way to eat it is with pitta and chips, and with an extra squeeze of lemon on the souvlaki.

4 garlic cloves, crushed

1 tablespoon dried oregano, plus extra to garnish

1 tablespoon white wine vinegar

125 ml/½ cup extra virgin olive oil

1 kg/2¼ lb. pork tenderloin, cut into 2-cm/¾-in. pieces

500 ml/generous 2 cups lager

½ bunch of fresh sage, leaves picked

sea salt and black pepper

TO SERVE

lemon wedges

sliced red onion

sweet potato chips

8 Yogurt Pittas (see page 170)

green pepper pickle

Greek yogurt

chilli sauce

Lemon Oregano Dressing (see page 164)

metal skewers

SERVES 4

Pound the garlic and oregano in a mortar and pestle with a pinch of salt until a coarse paste forms. Transfer to a large bowl, add the vinegar and oil and stir to combine. Add the pork and toss the pieces until well coated. Add the lager and leave to marinate for a minimum of 1 hour or overnight in the refrigerator for best results.

When ready to cook, thread the marinated pork pieces onto metal skewers, adding sage leaves between each the piece as you go.

Heat a char-grill pan over a medium-high heat. Cook the pork skewers on the char-grill, turning occasionally, for about 8–10 minutes until browned and cooked through. Season to taste and set aside to rest for 5 minutes.

Scatter the pork skewers with some extra oregano and serve with lemon wedges, sweet potato chips, Yogurt Pittas, green pepper pickle, Greek yogurt and the lightly pickled onion.

mustards & spices

Mustard was prized by the Ancient Egyptians, Greeks and Romans for the way it enhanced fish and meats, and it was found on every Roman dining table in the first century AD. The greatest philosophers of the era attributed it with an ability to inflame the senses, making it a very popular condiment in Roman times. Apicius, a Roman gourmet and lover of luxury, was already creating mustard-based sauces to serve with poultry, ostrich and sausages in the first century AD. When the Romans invaded today's France, they brought with them a taste for mustard; later, the then Emperor recommended growing this spice in all his estates, particularly in the gardens adjoining the monasteries on the outskirts of Paris.

The basic way of making mustard as the condiment that we know and love today is to combine the ground seeds of the mustard plant with liquid. The mustard varieties depend on the seeds and type of liquid used in the combination. There are three types of mustard plants: the white/yellow mustard (which have a less pungent flavour), black mustard and brown/Indian mustard (both with a more pungent flavour). White/yellow mustard seeds result into a mild paste, while brown and black seeds make a much hotter mustard. The temperature of the water and concentration of acids – like vinegar – also determine the strength of a prepared mustard. Mustards made with vinegar will have a long-lasting, slow burn, while those made with less acidic liquids, like pure water, will be extremely pungent when freshly prepared, but lose that punch more quickly. Although there are many mustards as condiments, the most popular are wholegrain and Dijon.

Ancient Greeks also imported Eastern spices (such as pepper, cassia, cinnamon and ginger) to the Mediterranean area. They also consumed many spices produced in neighbouring countries. Examples include caraway and poppy seeds for bread, fennel for vinegar sauces, coriander as a condiment in food and wine, and mint as a flavouring in meat sauces. Garlic was widely used by the country people in much of their cooking. Ancient Greeks wore parsley and marjoram as a crown at their feasts in an attempt to prevent drunkenness.

Spices and herbs played an important role in Ancient Greek medical science. Hippocrates wrote about spices and herbs, including saffron, cinnamon, thyme, coriander/cilantro, mint and marjoram. He noted that great care should be given to the preparation of herbs for medical use. Of the 400 herbal remedies utilized by Hippocrates, at least half are still in use today.

The Romans were extravagant users of spices and herbs. Spice-flavoured wines were used in Ancient Rome and spice-scented balms and oils were popular for use after the bath. Since spices were considered to have health properties, they were also used in poultices and healing plasters. When the Roman Empire extended to the northern side of the Alps, the peoples of those regions were introduced to pepper and other spices from the East.

Today an array of spices are used in the cuisines of the Mediterranean, although the further east you travel the more complex the spice mixture is. Based on ingredients introduced via the Spice Routes, common spices and herbs used in the Mediterranean include basil, bay leaf, black pepper, cloves, coriander/cilantro, cumin, dill, fennel, garlic, lavender, marjoram, mint, oregano, paprika, parsley, rosemary, saffron, sage, savory, sumac, tarragon, thyme and turmeric. Usage can be regional – for example, turmeric is a very eastern Mediterranean spice, so places in Northern Greece and Italy would not utilize this, but as you head into the Eastern Mediterranean region, with its North African influences, this becomes a widely used spice.

ONE-PAN TOMATO & CHICKEN ORZO

A childhood favourite, every Greek would have eaten a version of this with either meat or chicken. The chicken is slow-cooked in a rich tomato sauce and before the end of the cooking process the orzo is added, allowing it to absorb all the cooking juices to make a very tasty all-in-one dish.

125 ml/½ cup olive oil
800 g/1¾ lb. skinless boneless
   chicken thighs, halved
1 onion, finely chopped
1 carrot, finely chopped
1 celery stick, finely chopped
1 leek, finely chopped
2 fresh bay leaves
1–2 cinnamon sticks
1 tablespoon sundried tomato
   paste
1 quantity of Tomato Sauce
   (see page 150)
1 litre/4 cups chicken stock
   or water
300 g/1¾ cups orzo
sea salt and black pepper

TO SERVE (OPTIONAL)
sliced red onions
chilli/hot red pepper flakes
reserved celery fronds
basil leaves
freshly squeezed lemon juice

SERVES 4

Heat a third of the olive oil in a large ovenproof pan over a medium-high heat. Add the chicken and stir occasionally until well browned on all sides, then remove from the pan and set aside. Add the remaining olive oil and the onion and sauté until translucent. Add the carrot, celery and leek and cook for a further 10 minutes. Add the bay leaves, cinnamon sticks and sundried tomato paste and stir together.

Tip the chicken back into the pan and add the tomato sauce and stock or water. Bring to the boil and reduce the heat to a simmer for about 30 minutes.

Preheat the oven to 160°C fan/180°C/350°F/gas 4.

Tip the orzo into the ovenproof pan, give it a stir and season to taste. Bake in the preheated oven, covered, for about 10 minutes until the orzo has cooked, topping up with more stock or water for the orzo if needed. Take the pan out of the oven, scatter the red onions, chilli flakes, reserved celery fronds and basil leaves, and add a sprinkling of lemon juice to serve.

HERBES DE PROVENCE ROASTED CHICKEN ON CRISPY POTATOES & ONIONS *with*
soft buttery salad & mustard vinaigrette

The best way to cook a roast chicken is on a bed of potatoes. As the chicken cooks, the juices get absorbed by the potatoes for a super flavourful dish. Herbes de Provence traditionally includes dried thyme, basil, rosemary, tarragon, savory, marjoram, oregano, bay leaf and sometimes lavender. This roast is served with a buttery lettuce salad and a mustard vinaigrette – the ultimate comfort food.

2 tablespoons olive oil

4 tablespoons unsalted butter, melted

1 tablespoon dried herbes de Provence

1 kg/2¼ lb. Desiree potatoes, thinly sliced

1.8 kg/4 lb. chicken

2 onions, thinly sliced

4 fresh thyme sprigs, leaves picked

4 fresh rosemary sprigs

100 g/3½ oz. mixed butterhead lettuce and lambs lettuce

bunch of spring onions/scallions, thinly sliced

sea salt and black pepper

MUSTARD VINAIGRETTE

1 teaspoon Dijon mustard

1 teaspoon wholegrain mustard

pinch of sugar

2 tablespoons white wine vinegar

90–100 ml/6–7 tablespoons extra virgin olive oil

SERVES 4

Preheat the oven to 180°C fan/200°C/400°F/gas 6.

Mix the olive oil, butter and herbes de Provence in a bowl. Place the potatoes in a large bowl, add half the herb butter mixture and toss to coat. Season with salt and pepper.

Coat the chicken with the other half of the herb butter mixture.

Place the chicken in the centre of a roasting pan and arrange the potatoes around. Scatter the rosemary over the top. Roast in the preheated oven for 50–60 minutes until the potatoes are golden brown and crisp and a probe thermometer inserted into the thickest part of the chicken breasts registers 155°C/311°F (temperature will climb to 165°C/329°F as the chicken rests). Leave the chicken to rest for at least 20 minutes, and up to 45 minutes.

To make the dressing, whisk the mustards and the sugar into the vinegar in a bowl and season well. While whisking, gradually drizzle in the oil to form a thick dressing.

When ready to serve, place all the salad leaves and the spring onions in a bowl and dress with the vinaigrette.

Transfer the chicken to a cutting board and carve. Serve with the crispy potatoes and buttery salad.

SLOW-COOKED LAMB *with*
braised butter beans & black olives

Gently spiced slow-cooked lamb that falls off the bone, with butter beans in the juices, and so delicious served with green beans in a shallot and sherry dressing. The perfect family-friendly meal, but also lovely to feed a crowd.

1 leg of lamb (about 2 kg/4½ lb.)

1 tablespoon olive oil

2 onions, roughly chopped

4 carrots, roughly chopped

3 celery sticks, chopped

4 garlic cloves, bruised

500 ml/2 cups chicken stock

700-g/25-oz. jar of large Spanish butter/lima beans, rinsed and drained

460-g/1-lb. jar of roasted red (bell) peppers, drained and roughly chopped

200 g/7 oz. Spanish black olives, stoned/pitted

400 g/14 oz. green beans

handful of fresh parsley

sea salt and black pepper

SPICE MIX

4 garlic cloves, crushed

1 tablespoon hot smoked paprika

4 tablespoons olive oil

3 fresh rosemary sprigs, leaves picked and chopped

4 fresh thyme sprigs, leaves picked

VINAIGRETTE

1 medium shallot, finely chopped

1 teaspoon Dijon mustard

1½ tablespoons sherry wine vinegar

60 ml/¼ cup extra virgin olive oil

SERVES 4–6

To make the spice mix, in a small bowl combine all of the ingredients together with a large pinch of salt. Slash the lamb leg all over with a sharp knife and rub in. If you have the time, leave to marinate in the fridge for up to 24 hours, but this is not essential.

Preheat the oven to 130°C fan/150°C/300°F/gas 2.

Heat the oil in a roasting pan over a medium-high heat, add the onions, carrots, celery and garlic and sizzle for 5 minutes until the vegetables have softened. Pour over the stock and bring to the boil. Nestle the lamb in the pan, cover and roast in the preheated oven for 2½ hours.

Uncover the roasting pan and transfer the lamb to a plate using tongs. Stir the beans, peppers and olives through the stock in the pan, sit the lamb back on top and return to the oven, uncovered, for 1½ hours until the lamb is soft and falling off the bone.

Meanwhile, blanch and refresh the green beans and set aside.

To make the vinaigrette, in a medium bowl combine the shallot, mustard and vinegar and whisk to combine. Slowly whisk in the olive oil until well combined and season with salt and pepper.

Transfer the lamb to a board and shred using 2 forks. Stir the parsley through the braised beans in the roasting pan before serving with the shredded lamb and the green beans.

BAKED CHICKEN *with Spanish-style rice*

This is Spanish-inspired baked chicken and rice. The Calasparra Spanish short-grain rice is infused with saffron and paprika, and the chicken thighs nestled amongst it. Finishing with the fresh crispy vegetables is the perfect way to take this to the table, ready for everyone to dig in.

1.8 kg/4 lb. chicken, jointed

80 ml/⅓ cup olive oil

1½ onions, finely chopped

1 red (bell) pepper, finely chopped

1 green (bell) pepper, finely chopped

5 tomatoes, peeled and finely chopped

100 ml/generous ⅓ cup dry white wine

1.5 litres/quarts hot chicken stock

300 g/1½ cups Calasparra rice

4 garlic cloves

¼ teaspoon saffron threads

½ teaspoon sweet Spanish paprika

½ pack of fresh thyme

½ teaspoon black peppercorns

200 g/7 oz. cherry tomatoes on the vine

200 g/7 oz. mixed mangetout, green beans, sugarsnaps, cut into 3-cm/1¼-in. pieces

pea shoots, to garnish

sea salt and black pepper

SERVES 4

Thoroughly season the chicken with salt and black pepper. Heat the olive oil in a large heavy-based casserole/Dutch oven, add the chicken pieces, brown them for 4 minutes on each side, then remove and cover with foil. Add the onions to the casserole and cook for 10 minutes until soft but not coloured, then add the peppers and cook for 10 minutes until soft. Add the chopped tomatoes and cook for another 15 minutes.

Add the wine, bring to the boil, then add the hot stock and return the chicken to the dish. Increase the heat to medium, bring to the boil, then reduce the heat to low and simmer for 40 minutes or until stock has reduced by about a third.

Meanwhile, combine the garlic, saffron, paprika, thyme and peppercorns in a mortar and pestle and pound until well crushed. Add a few tablespoons of hot liquid from the casserole and mix well, then add the crushed spice mixture and the rice to the casserole and stir to combine. Bring to the boil, then simmer for 15–20 minutes until the rice is just tender and chicken is well cooked. Remove from the heat, add the cherry tomatoes on the vine and leave to stand for 10 minutes.

Blanch the mangetout, beans and sugarsnaps and refresh in cold water. Garnish with pea shoots and serve with the fresh green vegetables.

FOR THE TABLE: A LEISURELY SUMMER LUNCH

This is the style of lunch that goes on for hours, where the food is easy to make, looks impressive, is full of flavour and can be eaten warm or at room temperature. Each one of these dishes can stand alone as a main plate or a side dish, but are just fabulous when served as a spread to share. Make the schnitzels ahead, keep them in fridge and cook just before serving.

Pictured on pages 84–85

SCHNITZEL (VEAL & AUBERGINE)
with tangy tomato salsa

This recipe is for both a meat and a vegetable schnitzel, both of which are equally delicious and offer a Mediterranean twist on the traditional dish.

200 g/4 cups fresh fine
    breadcrumbs
2 tablespoons mixed fresh herbs,
    finely chopped (tarragon,
    parsley, basil)
75 g/½ cup plain/all-purpose flour
2 eggs, lightly beaten
4 veal schnitzels, ethically sourced
1 aubergine/eggplant, sliced
    lengthways
60 g/¼ cup butter
lemon wedges, to serve

TANGY TOMATO SALSA

1 ripe beef tomato, roughly
    chopped
2–3 gherkins, roughly chopped
1 red onion, finely chopped
squeeze of lemon juice
drizzle of olive oil

SERVES 4 TO SHARE

To make the tomato salsa, mix all the ingredients together in a bowl and set aside.

Mix the breadcrumbs with the mixed herbs in a shallow bowl. Place the flour and eggs in separate shallow bowls. Working with one piece of veal at a time, dip in the flour, then the egg, then the herby breadcrumbs to coat, shaking off excess between layers. Do the same with the aubergine slices, then set aside.

Heat a large frying pan/skillet over a medium-high heat and add half the butter. When foaming, add half the schnitzels and cook, turning once, for about 3–5 minutes until golden and cooked through. Transfer to a plate and keep warm. Wipe the pan clean with paper towels, then repeat with the remaining butter and schnitzels.

Serve with the tomato salsa.

PORK CUTLETS *with plums & basil*

Here, thickly sliced pork chops are cooked until lovely and tender
and served with a sweet, tangy and juicy plum sauce.

4 pork cutlets

2 tablespoons olive oil

3 plums, stoned/pitted, cut into
   5-mm/¼-in. slices

grated zest and juice of 1 lemon

1 tablespoon honey

½ teaspoon chilli/hot red pepper
   flakes

15 g/1 tablespoon butter

½ bunch of fresh basil leaves

sea salt and black pepper

SERVES 4

Season the pork generously with salt and pepper. Heat 1 tablespoon of the olive oil in a 30-cm/12-in. frying pan/skillet over a high heat until lightly smoking. Add the pork chops and cook for 4–6 minutes until the first side is nicely browned. Flip and continue to cook for about 3 minutes until the internal temperature registers 63°C/145°F on a thermometer. Transfer to a plate and cover with foil. Do not wipe out the pan.

Lower the heat to medium-low, add the remaining oil and the butter to the pan and add the plums, lemon juice and zest, honey, chilli flakes and some salt. Stir gently for about 2–3 minutes until the plums begin to soften but don't lose their shape. Place the pork chops on a serving platter, top with the plums and garnish with basil.

RICE WITH PANCETTA, PEAS & HERBS

The perfect side to serve with the Pork Cutlets (above), but this also makes
a lovely meal with the addition of a swirl of pesto or grated Parmesan.

200 g/generous 1 cup long-grain rice

30 g/1 oz. pine nuts

olive oil, for frying

200 g/7 oz. cubed pancetta

1 onion, finely chopped

1 garlic clove, crushed

1 green chilli/chile, finely chopped

freshly squeezed juice of 1 lemon

200 g/7 oz. peas, blanched and
   refreshed

½ bunch of fresh flat-leaf parsley,
   leaves picked and chopped

½ bunch of fresh mint, leaves
   picked

sea salt and black pepper

Pesto (see page 166), to serve
   (optional)

SERVES 4 TO SHARE

Cook the rice according to the pack instructions, drain and set aside.

Heat a frying pan/skillet over a medium-high heat. Add the pine nuts and toast for 1–2 minutes until golden. Remove the pine nuts to a small bowl.

Put the pan back over a medium-high heat, add a drizzle of oil and the pancetta and stir-fry for about 3 minutes until starting to brown. Add the onion, garlic and a pinch of salt and pepper. Stir the cooked rice into the mixture, along with the green chilli and the lemon juice. Cook for 2–3 minutes, then add the peas and herbs and serve with the pesto as a side or as a quick mid-week meal.

DUCK RAGÙ WITH PAPPARDELLE

*It is always surprising to me that Italians eat ragù dishes with pasta
in the middle of summer as we often think of it as a heartier dish.
This version, however, is lighter and fresher.*

2 tablespoons olive oil

4 duck legs

2 onions, finely chopped

2 garlic cloves, crushed

2 teaspoons ground cinnamon

2 teaspoons plain/all-purpose flour

250 ml/1 cup white wine

1 tablespoon sundried tomato
    paste

400-g/14-oz. can cherry tomatoes

1 vegetable stock cube, mixed with
    250 ml/1 cup hot water

3 fresh rosemary sprigs, leaves
    picked and chopped

2 bay leaves

1 teaspoon sugar

2 tablespoons milk

500 g/1 lb. 2oz. fresh pappardelle
    pasta

sea salt and black pepper

Parmesan and fresh basil, to serve

SERVES 4

Heat the oil in a large saucepan or casserole dish/Dutch oven over
a medium heat. Add the duck legs and brown on all sides for about
10 minutes. Remove to a plate and set aside.

Add the onions to the pan and cook for 5 minutes until softened. Add the
garlic and cook for a further 1 minute, then stir in the cinnamon and flour
and cook for a further minute. Return the duck legs to the pan, add the
wine, tomato paste, tomatoes, stock, herbs, sugar and seasoning. Bring
to a simmer, then lower the heat, cover with a lid and cook for 2 hours,
stirring every now and then.

Carefully lift the duck legs out of the sauce and place on a plate – they
will be very tender so try not to lose any of the meat. Pull off and discard
the fat, then shred the meat with 2 forks and discard the bones. Add
the meat back to the sauce with the milk and simmer, uncovered, for
a further 10–15 minutes while you cook the pasta.

Cook the pasta following the pack instructions, then drain, reserving
a cup of the pasta water, and add the pasta to the ragù. Stir to coat all
the pasta in the sauce and cook for 1 minute more, adding a splash of
cooking liquid if it looks dry. Serve with grated Parmesan and scattered
with fresh basil, if liked.

de hortu

FROM THE GARDEN

Vegetables

CUCUMBER & HERB GRAIN SALAD *with* *lemon & mint labneh balls & grape dressing*

Earthy grains, creamy labneh balls, fresh herbs, a red grape dressing and cucumber – all the best Mediterranean flavours that come together beautifully.

175 g/6 oz. bulgur wheat
1 vegetable stock cube
1 teaspoon dried oregano
1 romaine lettuce heart,
    roughly chopped
2 Lebanese cucumbers, shaved
    into ribbons
25 g/1 oz. fresh mint leaves,
    chopped, plus extra to serve
6 spring onions/scallions,
    thinly sliced
30 g/1 oz. pistachios, chopped
Lemon & Mint Labneh balls
    (see page 132)

RED GRAPE DRESSING
3 tablespoons extra virgin olive oil
200 g/7 oz. red grapes, thinly sliced
3 tablespoons runny honey
2 tablespoons red wine vinegar
sea salt and black pepper

SERVES 4

Place the bulgur wheat, stock cube and dried oregano in a large bowl and cover with plenty of boiling hot water. Stir to mix together and dissolve the stock cube. Soak for 10–20 minutes until just tender but still a little al dente. Drain well, then tip onto a clean tea/dish towel and leave for 15 minutes or so to remove as much excess water as you can.

Make the dressing. Heat 1 tablespoon of the olive oil in a frying pan/ skillet over a medium heat. Add the grapes and some seasoning and cook for 3 minutes. Add the remaining dressing ingredients and bring to the boil. Remove from the heat and set aside.

Tip the bulgur wheat into a mixing bowl. Stir in the lettuce, cucumber, mint, spring onions and grape dressing. Spoon onto a large serving platter and break over the minted labneh balls. Scatter over the pistachios and garnish with mint leaves. Serve straightaway while the lettuce is still crunchy.

WARM SAFFRON BABY POTATOES
with spinach, capers, lemon & yogurt

This is a lighter way to serve a potato salad that is still creamy but not gloopy or heavy. As the yogurt is swirled through whilst the potatoes are still warm, it melds well together, or allow to cool and serve as a great side for a barbecue.

500 g/1 lb. 2 oz. baby new potatoes

1 tablespoon olive oil

80 g/⅓ cup unsalted butter

1 onion, thinly sliced

pinch of saffron threads

100 g/3½ oz. spinach

2 tablespoons capers

grated zest and juice of 1 lemon

100 g/3½ oz. Greek yogurt

20 g/¾ oz. fresh dill, chopped

sea salt and black pepper

SERVES 4

Put the potatoes in a large saucepan and cover with cold salted water. Bring to the boil, then simmer for 15 minutes until they are tender but still hold their shape. Drain the potatoes and leave them to steam-dry.

Heat the oil with 1 tablespoon of the butter in a large frying pan/skillet over a medium-high heat. Once the butter is foaming, add the onion and saffron and cook for a few minutes, then turn the heat up and add the potatoes and fry for a few more minutes.

Add the remaining butter along with the spinach, capers, lemon zest and juice. Stir everything together for a few minutes so that the potatoes are coated and the spinach has wilted, then season to taste with salt and black pepper. Stir through the Greek yogurt and finish with dill to serve.

SPRING GREENS SALAD
with feta & mint dressing

This salad is so versatile and I guarantee you will want to make it time and time again. For a more substantial salad you can add some poached chicken. For extra flavour, halve the lettuce and lightly char in a griddle pan, just to add flavour but not to cook through. Or simply serve this as is.

150 g/5½ oz. sugarsnap peas,
    trimmed
150 g/5½ oz. green beans,
    trimmed and coarsely chopped
2 cucumbers, coarsely chopped
1 cos lettuce, coarsely chopped

FETA DRESSING
100 ml/generous ⅓ cup extra
    virgin olive oil
freshly squeezed juice of 1 lemon,
    or to taste
1 tablespoon sherry vinegar
1 garlic clove, finely grated
100 g/3½ oz. feta, crumbled
½ bunch of fresh mint, leaves torn

SERVES 4 AS A SIDE

For the feta dressing, shake the oil, lemon, vinegar and garlic in a screwtop jar or small bowl to combine. Season to taste, add the feta and refrigerate until needed.

Blanch the sugarsnap peas and beans in a pan of boiling water until bright green and just tender. Drain, refresh in iced water, then drain well and toss in a bowl with cucumber and lettuce. Store in an airtight container until required.

To serve, toss the greens with the feta dressing in a serving bowl.

SALADE DE CAROTTES

This vibrant and refreshing carrot salad is a classic in France. Grated carrots are tossed with lemon juice, olive oil, mustard, honey, seasoning and some fresh herbs. The carrots can be finely or coarsely grated, depending on your preference.

2 tablespoons extra virgin olive oil
freshly squeezed juice of ½ lemon,
   or more to taste
1 teaspoon mustard
½ teaspoon runny honey
450 g/1 lb. carrots, peeled and grated
2 tablespoons finely chopped mixed
   fresh herbs (parsley, tarragon,
   chives or chervil)
sea salt and black pepper

SERVES 2

Stir together the olive oil, lemon juice, mustard, honey and a little salt in a mixing bowl. Add the carrots and chopped herbs and toss thoroughly with the dressing.

Taste, and season with additional lemon juice and salt and pepper if needed.

SALADE RACHEL

The French do make the most amazing salads. Salade Rachel originates from the region of Gironde and is a combination of celery, shaved truffles, artichokes, boiled potatoes, asparagus and mayonnaise. In my version the truffle has been mixed into the mayonnaise dressing.

½ head of celery, leaves picked
   and reserved
bunch of asparagus tips
freshly squeezed juice of 1 lemon
1 tablespoon truffles preserved in
   olive oil (or a few shavings of fresh
   summer truffle)
3 tablespoons mayonnaise
   (see page 158)
200 g/7 oz. new potatoes, boiled
   and cooled
1 frisée lettuce, leaves picked
sea salt and black pepper
drizzle of olive oil, to serve

SERVES 2

Start by boiling a large saucepan of water and blanching the celery sticks for a few minutes, then refresh them in iced water. Keep the water boiling and blanch, then refresh the asparagus.

Put the lemon juice, truffles in olive oil, mayonnaise and some salt and pepper in the base of a serving dish and mix together.

Thinly slice the blanched celery and add it to the serving dish on top of the truffle mayo mixture, followed by the new potatoes, asparagus tips and frisee lettuce. Finish with a drizzle of olive oil and serve with a glass of crisp white wine.

AUBERGINE TARTARE
with flat-leaf parsley salad

A flavour-packed super tasty alternative to steak tartare. A great side or starter, or serve as canapés for a crowd. It is also nice piled into a bowl with the bread on the side, for people to help themselves family style.

2 aubergines/eggplants,
   cut into small cubes
2 tablespoons olive oil,
   plus extra for brushing
20 thin baguette slices
2 tablespoons finely chopped
   mixed fresh herbs (chervil,
   parsley, tarragon)
1 teaspoon cornichons, finely
   chopped
1 teaspoon capers, finely chopped
1 teaspoon Dijon mustard
freshly squeezed juice of 1 lemon
1 teaspoon Dijon mustard
Tabasco sauce and parsley oil,
   to taste
sea salt and black pepper

PARSLEY SALAD
50 g/1¾ oz. fresh flat-leaf
   parsley, coarsely torn
15 ml/1 tablespoon extra virgin
   olive oil
3 spring onions/scallions,
   thinly sliced
freshly squeezed juice of ½ lemon

SERVES 4 TO SHARE

Preheat the oven to 160°C fan/180°C/350°F/gas 4. Line a baking sheet with non-stick baking paper.

Place the aubergine in a single layer on the lined baking sheet, season well with salt and pepper and drizzle with olive oil. Bake in the preheated oven for 20–25 minutes until golden brown.

Brush the baguette slices with olive oil, season to taste and bake, turning once, for 5–7 minutes until golden and crisp. Set aside to cool.

For the parsley salad, combine all the ingredients in a bowl, toss lightly to combine and set aside.

Put the roasted aubergine in a large bowl with the remaining ingredients, stir to combine and season to taste. Pile the onto the toasted crostini, top with parsley salad (or serve alongside) and serve.

olive oil & olives

Olive oil is made by pressing fresh olives to extract the oil. It's a popular cooking oil that is produced in olive-growing regions, most often France, Italy, Spain and Greece, as well as some new-world countries. The oil is used in cooking, cosmetics, medicine, soaps, and as a fuel for traditional lamps. In the Mediterranean regions, olive oil multitasks as a dip for bread, for drizzling on pasta, for use in cooking, or as part of a salad dressing. Its flavour is highly prized and it is one of the healthier fats. The benefits of olive oil, especially extra virgin olive oil, are numerous – it contains vitamins A and E, unsaturated fatty acids and important bisphenols (they give a bitter taste and are powerful antioxidants). The minerals it contains include calcium, magnesium, phosphorus, potassium, iron and zinc. The combination of this oil's properties has a beneficial effect on the health and condition of the cardiovascular system.

EXTRA VIRGIN OLIVE OIL This is the least- processed, most rich-tasting olive oil. Quality cold-pressed should have an acidity level of 0.8% or less. A good extra virgin olive oil is also rich in polyphenols, which have important antioxidant and anti-inflammatory properties.

VIRGIN OLIVE OIL This is quite similar to extra virgin olive oil. However, virgin olive oil is slightly lower in quality, and has an acidity around 1.5%.

PURE OLIVE OIL (OR OLIVE OIL) When the term 'pure' is used, it is meant to tell you that the bottle contains only olive oil. However, it can be a blend of virgin oils (about 15–20%) and the remaining 80–85% or so would likely be refined olive oils. These are usually lighter-tasting oils.

LIGHT OLIVE OIL The word 'light' refers to the flavour. Like pure olive oil, light olive oil is a blend of oils with a higher smoking point than extra virgin olive oil.

When choosing and olive oil, look at the name, origin and packaging to be sure of what you are buying.

THE NAME Ensure that the label clearly states that the product is cold-pressed extra virgin olive oil (if that is what you are looking for). Light olive oil, pure olive oil, refined olive oil, etc are further processed and are typically blends of different olive oils.

ACIDITY LEVEL A true extra virgin olive oil must have an acidity of less than 0.8%, while the highest quality extra virgin olive oils will have an acidity of 0.3% or less. Product acidity is not usually printed on labels, but should be easily located on a company's website. the exact olives used in making the oil.

THE OLIVES When the specific origin and type of olive is not listed, the olive oil is likely produced from many different olives from different groves and different parts of the world, versus olives of a single region or single estate.

THE PACKAGING Buy olive oils packaged in dark glass bottles or cans. This is important because olive oil can deteriorate when exposed to light.

Olives range from simple to complex, from a basic black to a vibrant green, from very mild to super salty. They can be eaten alone or incorporated into recipes. It may surprise you to learn that the only difference between green olives and black olives is ripeness – unripe olives are green, whereas fully ripe olives are black (see page 165). Because the raw green olives have a naturally bitter taste, they need to be cured. This can be done through various methods including oil-curing, water-curing, brining, dry-curing, or placing in a lye solution. Unopened olives can be stored at room temperature for up to 2 years. Opened olives should be refrigerated in their own liquid in a non-metal container and will last for 1 to 2 months after opening.

CARROT, PARMESAN & BASIL FRITTERS

Fritters are a magical way of eating vegetables, and here they are further enhanced by the flavour bomb additions of cheese and fresh herbs.

1 tablespoon olive oil, plus extra
    for shallow frying
1 small onion, thinly sliced
1 garlic clove, crushed
200 g/7 oz. coarsely grated carrot
100 g/1⅓ cups coarsely grated
    Parmesan
100 g/¾ cup plain/all-purpose flour
2 tablespoons chopped fresh sage,
    plus extra leaves to serve
1 tablespoon chopped fresh thyme
grated zest of 1 lemon
sea salt and black pepper
lemon wedges, to serve
Saffron Aïoli (see page 159), to serve

SERVES 4–6 TO SHARE

Heat the oil in a saucepan over a medium-high heat. Add the onion and garlic and sauté for 3–4 minutes until tender. Tip into a large bowl, add the carrot, Parmesan, flour, herbs and lemon zest, season to taste and mix well. Form into 10–12 patties and set aside on a tray.

Heat 1 cm/½ in. oil in a frying pan/skillet over a medium-high heat, add the sage leaves and fry until crisp. Drain on paper towels.

Add the patties to the pan in batches and fry for 5–6 minutes until golden brown on both sides and cooked through. Drain on paper towels, season to taste and serve topped with the sage leaves with lemon wedges and saffron aïoli.

COURGETTE & HALLOUMI FRITTERS

Here is a perfect recipe for using up a glut of courgettes/zucchini from your allotment or garden, or even lurking in your fridge. This brilliant method of pan-frying them ensures they are nice and crispy.

400 g/14 oz. courgettes/zucchini
    trimmed, coarsely grated
250 g/9 oz. halloumi, diced
2 small eggs, lightly beaten
½ bunch each of fresh parsley, mint,
    basil and dill, finely chopped,
    plus extra basil to garnish
100 g/¾ cup plain/all-purpose flour
80 ml/⅓ cup olive oil
sea salt
lemon wedges, to serve

SERVES 4–6 TO SHARE

Combine the courgette and halloumi in a bowl, add the eggs, herbs, flour and a pinch of salt and mix well.

Heat 1 tablespoon of the oil in a frying pan/skillet over a medium-high heat. Add heaped spoonfuls of the courgette mixture in batches and fry, turning occasionally and adding extra oil with each batch, for 3–4 minutes until golden. Drain on paper towels, then serve warm with lemon wedges.

ROASTED VEGETABLE & ORECCHIETTE SALAD
with a tomato & caper dressing

This is the easiest most versatile pasta salad. In fact it's a hybrid – it can be eaten as a hot pasta dish which is sweet and sour with the tomato caper dressing with loads of cheese or allowed to cool and be eaten as a side salad, perfect for a barbecue.

300 g/10½ oz. orecchiette pasta
1 large aubergine/eggplant,
    cut into 5-mm/¼-in. slices
1 courgette/zucchini, cut into
    5-mm/¼-in. slices
1 yellow (bell) pepper, cut into
    5-mm/¼-in. strips
3 garlic cloves
3 tablespoons olive oil
2 tablespoons sultanas/golden
    raisins
small bunch of fresh basil,
    leaves picked
2 handfuls of rocket/arugula
grated zest of ½ lemon
    (juice reserved for dressing)
2 tablespoons pine nuts
20 g/¾ oz. pecorino, shaved
sea salt and black pepper

TOMATO CAPER DRESSING
4 tablespoons Tomato Sauce
    (see page 150)
2 teaspoons capers, drained and
    chopped
freshly squeezed juice of ½ lemon
1 tablespoon balsamic vinegar
5 tablespoons olive oil

SERVES 4

Preheat the oven to 200°C fan/220°C/425°F/gas 7.

Cook the pasta following the pack instructions, then drain, rinse under cold running water until cool, then drain again.

Place all the vegetables in a roasting pan with the garlic and drizzle with oil. Season well with salt and pepper. Roast the vegetables in the preheated oven for 20 minutes. Toss everything together and return to the oven for a further 5–10 minutes, or until hot. Remove from the oven and leave to cool.

In a bowl, mix the dressing ingredients and taste for seasoning. Place the dressing in the base of a serving bowl, add the cooked pasta and roasted vegetables and mix through the dressing. Top with the sultanas, basil, rocket, lemon zest, pine nuts and pecorino.

FOR THE TABLE: A CELEBRATION OF SUMMER VEGETABLES

Here is a selection of vegetable-based dishes that are both colourful and flavourful. Perfect for feeding a crowd at a summer garden party and not just for vegetarians and vegans – these recipes will appeal to all lovers of fresh produce and good ingredients, prepared simply.

Pictured on pages 106–107

MARINATED SUMMER VEGETABLES

A super versatile plate of vegetables that can work as a side or as an alternative to crudités. They also can be transformed into a lovely salad topped with crumbled cheese that melds into the flavour. They look great as part of a vegetarian spread or a large feasting table.

100 g/3½ oz. cherry tomatoes, roasted
100 g/3½ oz. baby carrots, peeled and cooked
100 g/3½ oz. baby peas, blanched and partly husked
100 g/3½ oz. baby courgettes/ zucchini, blanched
8 baby field mushrooms, roasted
8 baby fennel, thinly sliced
100 ml/⅓ cup plus 1 tablespoon extra virgin olive oil
grated zest and juice of 1 lemon
1 garlic clove, finely grated
3 fresh thyme sprigs, leaves picked
sea salt and black pepper

TO SERVE
Marinated Goat's Cheese with charred sourdough (see opposite)
Pan-fried Baby Potatoes with olives (see opposite)

SERVES 4 TO SHARE

Place all the vegetables in a large bowl with the olive oil, lemon zest and juice, garlic, thyme and season with salt and pepper. Leave to marinate at room temperature for 10 minutes.

Serve with the marinated goat's cheese and pan-fried potatoes.

PAN-FRIED BABY POTATOES
with garlic, sage & olives

A very simple side dish that can go with anything. These humble ingredients are transformed when slowly pan fried and create a lovely potato dish that is delicious and super versatile.

80 ml/⅓ cup extra virgin olive oil
600 g/1 lb. 5 oz. baby potatoes
8 garlic cloves, unpeeled
200 g/7 oz. mixed olives, stoned/ pitted
6 fresh sage leaves
shaved preserved lemon (optional)

SERVES 4 TO SHARE

Heat the olive oil in a frying pan/skillet over a low heat. Add the potatoes and garlic and cook, stirring occasionally for about 30 minutes until tender and golden. Add the olives and cook for a further 10 minutes, then add the sage and cook until crisp. Scatter over the preserved lemon, if using, and serve.

MARINATED GOAT'S CHEESE
with charred sourdough

Once you have tried these marinated goat's cheese balls, you will always have a batch in your fridge. They can be a starter on a sharing board, a quick snack, top any roasted vegetables, spread on a toastie... The list is endless.

400 ml/scant 1¾ cups olive oil
400 g/14 oz. soft rindless goat's cheese
3 pared strips of lemon zest
3 fresh thyme sprigs
2 fresh rosemary sprigs
2 red chillies, pierced a few times with a sharp knife
1 teaspoon fennel seeds
charred sourdough, to serve

2 x 500-g/1 lb. 2-oz. jars

MAKES 2 JARS

Sterilize the 2 jars (see page 4).

Oil your hands well, then break the goat's cheese into small pieces and roll into balls. Place the cheese in the jar, then pack the lemon zest, thyme, rosemary and chillies around the cheese. Scatter over the fennel seeds and pour over the oil.

Leave to marinate in the fridge for 2 days. Serve with toasted sourdough. Store in the fridge, and eat within 2 weeks.

BRAISED BROAD BEANS & PEAS
with mint & trofie pasta

*A light summer bowl of pasta, gently braised with broad/fava beans
and peas for gentle, delicate flavours. This is easily made into a vegan
dish by using vegan cheese.*

about 1 kg/2¼ lb. broad/fava
    beans, podded (250 g/9 oz.
    podded weight)
150 g/5½ oz. frozen garden peas
300 g/10½ oz. trofie pasta
2 tablespoons olive oil
8 thin pancetta slices (optional)
2 garlic cloves, crushed
50 ml/3½ tablespoons white wine
100 ml/generous ⅓ cup vegetable
    stock
3 tablespoons fresh mint leaves,
    finely chopped, plus extra to
    garnish
4 tablespoons grated Parmesan
    (or a vegan option)
black pepper

SERVES 4

Cook the broad beans and peas in a large saucepan of boiling salted water for 2–3 minutes until tender. Scoop them into a sieve with a slotted spoon (reserving the water), then refresh under cold water. Bring the water back to the boil and cook the pasta according to the pack instructions.

Meanwhile, remove and discard the outer skin from the broad beans, and set aside with the peas.

Heat the olive oil in a frying pan/skillet over a medium heat and cook the pancetta slices, if using, for 4–6 minutes until golden and crispy. Transfer to a plate lined with paper towels.

In the same pan, add the garlic and white wine and cook down for a few minutes, then add the vegetable stock and cook for a few more minutes. Add the podded broad beans and peas and cook gently for 1 minute.

Drain the pasta and return to the saucepan. Tip in the broad bean mixture and add the mint and half the Parmesan, tossing together. Break up the pancetta if using and toss into the pasta.

Serve in bowls scattered with the remaining Parmesan, a grind of black pepper and some mint leaves to garnish.

ex agro

FROM THE FIELD
Grains & pulses

FREGOLA WITH COURGETTES, CORN, BASIL & RICOTTA

Sometimes called Sardinian couscous, fregola lands somewhere between a grain and a pasta, with a nutty flavour and irregular texture that's all its own. Use it where you would couscous or orzo, adding a toasted dimension to hot and cold side dishes. This is one of those dishes that can be eaten warm or at room temperature with a dollop of ricotta.

200 g/7 oz. fregola

3 tablespoons olive oil

1 shallot, finely chopped

2 courgettes/zucchini, cut into rounds

3 garlic cloves, crushed

pinch of Aleppo chilli/hot red pepper flakes

2 corn on the cob, kernels shaved

30 g/1 oz. Manchego, shaved, plus extra to garnish

15–20 fresh basil leaves, plus extra to garnish

grated zest and juice of 1 lemon

sea salt and black pepper

RICOTTA

250-g/9-oz. block of ricotta

2 tablespoons olive oil

1 tablespoon runny honey

1 teaspoon dried oregano

1 teaspoon Aleppo chilli/hot red pepper flakes

SERVES 4

Cook the fregola in a large saucepan of boiling water according to the pack instructions, then drain and set aside to cool, reserving about 250 ml/1 cup of the cooking water.

Heat 2 tablespoons of the oil in a large sauté pan over a medium heat. Add the shallot and courgettes and some salt and pepper and cook for a few minutes. Add the garlic and chilli flakes and cook for a few more minutes until the garlic is fragrant. Add the corn and continue sautéing for 5–6 minutes until the corn is tender, but still a little snappy.

Add the cooked fregola to the courgette mixture, drizzle with another tablespoon of olive oil and stir in the Manchego, basil and lemon zest. Add 60–120 ml/¼–½ cup of the pasta water to loosen, and more if you prefer it more 'saucy'. Garnish with fresh basil and an extra sprinkling of Manchego.

Place the block of ricotta on a serving dish and drizzle with olive oil and runny honey., then finish with the oregano and chilli flakes. Serve alongside the fregola with courgettes, placing a few tablespoons into the mixture or letting guests help themselves.

GREEK-STYLE RICE
with spinach, leek dill & lemon

Rustic, comforting and a mid-week staple in every Greek home. Simply serve with a chunk of feta and olives, this dish can be made with a few variations – either just spinach or just leek, add some chopped tomatoes into it. I think the best combination is spinach, leek and dill for a dish that is both simple and life enhancing.

100 ml/⅓ cup plus 1 tablespoon Greek extra virgin olive oil

1 onion , finely chopped

2 leeks, thinly sliced

500 g/1 lb. 2 oz. baby spinach leaves, washed and finely chopped

bunch of fresh dill, finely chopped

300 g/1⅔ cups long-grain rice

freshly squeezed juice of 1–2 lemons

SERVES 4

Heat the oil in a large saucepan over a medium heat. Add the onion and leeks and gently cook for 10 minutes until softened but not coloured. Add the spinach and half the dill and cook over a high heat, stirring regularly, until the spinach has wilted down and all the liquid has evaporated.

Stir in the rice, add 600 ml/2½ cups water and bring to the boil. Turn the heat right down again to a very gentle simmer, cover the pan with a tight-fitting lid and cook for 25–30 minutes or until the rice has cooked and absorbed all the water. Give it a stir after 15 minutes to ensure even cooking, adding a drop more water as required.

When the rice is cooked, stir in the remaining dill, season well, squeeze over the lemon juice to taste and serve.

fresh herbs

Common herbs found throughout the Mediterranean region include basil, bay leaf, chervil, chives, coriander/cilantro dill, fennel, lavender, marjoram, mint, oregano (Italian, Greek), parsley, rosemary, saffron, sage, savory, tarragon and thyme. They lend flavour, colour and vital micro nutrients to Mediterranean cooking, and are an important ingredient in many of the recipes in this book.

PARSLEY is first on this list because it's useful in so many dishes, pretty much everyone loves it and it's a nutrition superstar. Useful as a digestive aid and natural breath freshener, its bright green leaves are packed with vitamins C, B12 and A, as well as good amounts of potassium. It is perfect with meat, fish, vegetarian dishes and salads – a great all-rounder.

THYME is one of the herbs holds up best to drying. It's very easy to grow and works really well fresh and dried in recipes. Besides its lovely flavour, thyme is a powerful antioxidant and a natural antibacterial and antimicrobial agent. A vinaigrette made with thyme will kill additional germs – which is why thyme has long been used as a preservative herb as well.

BASIL in its dried form is great in sauce bases but it is also one of the most popular herbs to use fresh. The iconic Italian caprese salad, with plenty of fresh basil, ripe tomatoes, mozzarella cheese, balsamic vinegar, olive oil, salt and pepper, is what it is best known for.

ROSEMARY will grow almost anywhere you plant it and, in addition to the flavourful, needle-like evergreen leaves, it bears pretty blue flowers that bees love. Its pine-meets-floral flavour is usually associated with chicken dishes, but it's equally delicious chopped and mixed with olive oil, then drizzled over potatoes and veggies. Rosemary also enhances savoury baked goods.

OREGANO is related to marjoram and is a hardy, perennial herb that comes in many flavour varieties, from peppery to lemony to burn-your-tongue hot. Usually more flavourful when dried than fresh, oregano is the star of Greek salads and most Italian cuisine (you really can't have a good pizza without it). Oregano is another herb that's high in antioxidants, and it's used to treat stomach ailments, especially digestive issues.

SAGE has an especially long and beloved history, having been written about by Pliny the Elder as he reported that it is a diuretic and a tonic. Modern cooks have found plenty more uses for the peppery-flavoured leaves, including pairing with white beans for a hummus-like dip, adding whole leaves into fresh pasta dishes, and infusing into honey.

The best way to store the soft herbs for longevity is to start by removing rubber bands or fastenings (if store bought). Wash the herbs in cool water, then dry the leaves very well by giving them a good shake or putting them in a salad spinner and giving them a gentle spin. Place them on paper towels and pat the herbs dry and roll the towels over them so that you can capture any remaining moisture.

Put the herbs in water (like a bouquet of flowers). Fill a large glass of water a third full and put the herbs in it, like a bouquet of flowers, with only the stems not any of the leaves in water. Cover the herb leaves with a plastic bag. This process should keep them fresh for up to 5 days.

For the stronger herbs such as rosemary and thyme, wrap the sprigs in a clean damp kitchen cloth or paper towel, then in a layer of clingfilm/plastic wrap or put in a ziplock bag. This way they can be refrigerated for up to a week and maintain their freshness.

CAMARGUE RICE SALAD
with pan-fried apricots & halloumi

Apricots and halloumi pair beautifully in this dish of tangy sweet with salty cheese and earthy red Camargue rice. Camargue rice is grown in the eponymous region of southeastern France, and it features a beautiful red russet colour and wonderful nutty flavour.

250 g/1⅓ cups Camargue rice

250 g/9 oz. halloumi , cut into strips

4 tablespoons olive oil

3–4 apricots, stoned/pitted and chopped

1 tablespoon brown sugar

1 tablespoon red wine vinegar

100 g/3½ oz. baby spinach

2 celery sticks, thinly sliced

50 g/1¾ oz. toasted pine nuts

DRESSING

1 teaspoon Dijon mustard

1 teaspoon honey

30 ml/2 tablespoons red wine vinegar

60 ml/¼ cup olive oil

1 teaspoon chilli/hot red pepper flakes (optional)

SERVES 4 TO SHARE

Cook the rice according to the pack instructions, leave to cool, then place on a serving platter.

Heat a non-stick frying pan/skillet over a medium heat. Add the halloumi and cook for 5–7 minutes, turning halfway, until the halloumi is golden. Remove from the pan. Add 1 tablespoon of the olive oil and pan-fry the apricots for 2–3 minutes until they soften, then turn them over and add the brown sugar and red wine vinegar. Return the halloumi to the pan.

Stir the spinach leaves into the rice, then add the celery and spoon the halloumi and apricot mixture, with all the juices, onto the rice on the platter. Finish with the pine nuts.

Make the dressing by mixing all the ingredients together in a small bowl or jar and serve alongside the rice and halloumi.

HONEYED HERITAGE CARROT & BABY BEET GRAIN PLATTER *with tarragon*

A pretty platter of roasted vegetables on a bed of grains to absorb all the juices and finished with tarragon. The pungent, bittersweet flavour of tarragon is often compared to liquorice, anise and fennel, and it really lifts the earthiness of this dish. You could easily top this with some of the marinated goat's cheese balls from page 105 for extra creaminess.

200 g/7 oz. baby beetroot/beet, scrubbed and halved
60 g/¼ cup unsalted butter
60 ml/¼ cup olive oil
300 g/10½ oz. heritage carrots, halved if large
3 garlic cloves, crushed
3 fresh tarragon sprigs
2 fresh thyme sprigs
1 fresh rosemary sprig
½ teaspoon mustard seeds
½ teaspoon cumin seeds
2 tablespoons honey
2 tablespoons apple cider vinegar
100 ml/generous ⅓ cup vegetable stock
200 g/7 oz. cooked grains
sea salt and black pepper
fresh tarragon and parsley, to serve

SERVES 4

Preheat the oven to 160°C fan/180°C/350°F/gas 4.

Place the baby beetroot on a baking sheet and dot with half the butter and half the olive oil. Season well and roast for 30–40 minutes, or until cooked through.

In a large, deep sauté pan, melt the remaining butter in the olive oil. Add the carrots, garlic, tarragon, thyme, rosemary and mustard and cumin seeds and season with salt and pepper. Cook over a medium heat, stirring occasionally, for about 12 minutes until the carrots are golden. Add the honey and cook, stirring, for about 3 minutes until the honey is lightly caramelized. Stir in the vinegar and cook for about 2 minutes until the carrots are evenly coated. Add the stock, cover and cook over a medium-low heat, stirring occasionally, for about 20 minutes until the carrots are tender and the liquid is syrupy. Transfer the carrots to a plate, discarding the herb sprigs, and leave to cool slightly.

To serve, place the cooked grains on a platter and top with the baby beetroot with their juices, carrots and juices and the fresh herbs.

GRILLED TOMATOES, GRAIN & LENTIL MIX *with*
pickled cucumber dressing & sourdough croutons

A great way to use the last bits of your sourdough and ripe tomatoes.
The grilled tomatoes release their juices to add to the dressing on a bed
of grains and lentils, topped with a pickled cucumber dressing for some
extra zing. You will make this dish again and again.

6 firm vine-ripened tomatoes

6 Roma tomatoes, halved

3 tablespoons olive oil, plus extra
    to finish

3 thick sourdough bread slices,
    cut into squares

1 garlic clove, crushed

1 tablespoon mixed seeds

1 tablespoon fresh parsley,
    finely chopped

200 g/7 oz. mixed lentils and grains

100 g/3½ oz. green olives, stoned/
    pitted and halved

6 Parma ham slices

sea salt and black pepper

PICKLED CUCUMBER DRESSING

40 ml/2½ tablespoons sherry
    vinegar

freshly squeezed juice of 1 lemon

80 ml/⅓ cup extra virgin olive oil

1 teaspoon dried oregano

drizzle of runny honey, or to taste

3 baby cucumbers, chopped

SERVES 4

Preheat the barbecue or griddle pan and preheat the oven to 160°C fan/ 180°C/350°F/gas 4.

Season the tomatoes well with salt and pepper and drizzle with 1 tablespoon of the olive oil.

Place the tomatoes on the hot barbecue, cover with a lid and cook over a high heat for 1–2 minutes, turning occasionally until tender and charred. Alternatively, place on a heated griddle pan and cook until charred on the outside and tender on the inside.

Meanwhile, make the pickled cucumber dressing. Whisk the sherry vinegar, lemon juice, olive oil, oregano and honey together in a bowl, add the chopped cucumber and leave to pickle for at least 30 minutes.

In a bowl mix the sourdough squares with the crushed garlic, mixed seeds, 2 tablespoons of the olive oil and season well. Spread out on a baking sheet and bake in the preheated oven for 8–10 minutes until golden and crisp. Mix with the chopped parsley and set aside.

In a serving dish, add the mixed lentils and grains, top with the tomatoes, olives, Parma ham and pickled cucumber, then top with croutons.

GRILLED AUBERGINE GRAIN BOWLS
with fresh borlotti beans & dill

If you can get fresh borlotti/cranberry beans in season, they are great with this baked aubergine, but using the canned version is just as nice. This is an excellent vegan dish to share with friends as part of a larger table. It is also great to make ahead and have for lunch, topped with green salad.

2 aubergines/eggplants, halved
  lengthways
1 tablespoon extra virgin olive oil
75 g/2¾ oz. quick-cook freekeh
  and quinoa
finely grated zest of 1 lemon
  and juice of ½
1 tablespoon raisins
200 g/7 oz. cherry tomatoes,
  halved
1 teaspoon chilli paste (such as
  harissa or a smoked chilli paste),
  plus extra to serve
50 g/1¾ oz. feta (optional)
½ x 20-g/¾-oz. pack fresh dill,
  roughly chopped
200 g/7 oz. fresh borlotti/
  cranberry beans, blanched
  and refreshed
sea salt and black pepper
2 tablespoons fat-free Greek
  yogurt, to serve (optional)

SERVES 4 TO SHARE

Preheat the grill/broiler to high (or light the barbecue).

Slash the aubergines in a criss-cross pattern through the flesh, but not the skin. Season and brush with ½ tablespoon of the oil. Place, skin side up, in a small roasting pan and grill/broil for 20 minutes, turning halfway through.

Meanwhile, boil the grains in a saucepan of water for 12–13 minutes, or until just tender. Drain well, then put into a bowl with the remaining oil, lemon zest and juice and raisins. Season. Add the cherry tomatoes to the aubergine dish and grill for another 10 minutes.

Mix the chilli paste, feta, if using, dill and borlotti beans into the grains, then serve with the aubergines. Add a spoon of yogurt on top if you wish and serve.

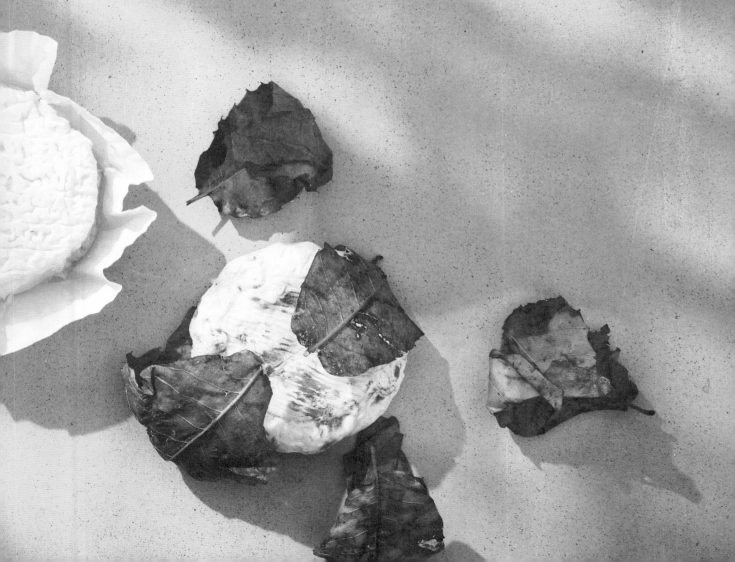

a lac
FROM THE DAIRY
Cheese & yogurt

BURRATA WITH BLISTERED PEACHES & HEIRLOOM TOMATOES

High-summer in-season fruit such as tomatoes, peaches and cherries should be celebrated. Simply blister the peaches and tomatoes, top with burrata and serve with a cherry dressing. The ingredients do all the work. See overleaf for the other dishes shown in the photo.

4 ripe peaches, halved and stoned/pitted

4 heirloom tomatoes, quartered

100 g/3½ oz. cherries, halved and stoned/pitted

50 g/1¾ oz. rocket/arugula leaves

10 g/3½ teaspoons pumpkin seeds/pepitas

4 x 125-g/4½-oz. burrata

fresh basil leaves, to serve

DRESSING

100 ml/generous ⅓ cup extra virgin olive oil

30 ml/2 tablespoons Champagne vinegar

1 tablespoon runny honey

1 garlic clove, crushed

grated zest and juice of 1 lemon

1 teaspoon dried oregano

pinch of chilli/hot red pepper flakes

1 fresh dill sprig, chopped

2 fresh parsley sprigs, chopped

SERVES 4

Preheat the barbecue or griddle pan to smoking.

Start by mixing all the dressing ingredients directly in a serving dish, then set aside until ready to use.

Place the peach halves on the hot grill or griddle skin side down and cook for 2–3 minutes (depending on their ripeness) until their skins blister, then turn to griddle their flesh. Transfer to the serving platter with the dressing. Do the same with the tomatoes, although these will be quicker to blister, then transfer to the serving dish. The juices will all start to meld nicely.

Add the cherries, then top with rocket leaves and pumpkin seeds. Mix just before serving and top with burrata and basil leaves.

BURRATA WITH COURGETTES & MINT

These courgettes/zucchini can be made a day before, brought to room temperature, then topped with mint and burrata.

500 g/1 lb. 2 oz. courgettes/
zucchini, cut diagonally into
2.5-cm/1-in. thick lengths
60 ml/¼ cup extra virgin olive oil,
plus extra to serve
2 garlic cloves – 1 clove cut into
4 slices and 1 finely chopped
20 g/1 oz. fresh mint, leaves picked
1 dried red chilli/chile, crushed
2 tablespoons red wine vinegar
4 x 125 g/4½ oz. burrata
sea salt and black pepper

SERVES 2

Line a baking sheet with kitchen paper. Place the courgettes on the sheet and stand to drain for at least 30 minutes. Pat dry with kitchen paper.

Place the oil and sliced garlic in a large frying pan/skillet over a medium heat and gently fry until golden brown. Remove the garlic with a slotted spoon and discard. Increase the heat to medium-high, add the courgettes in batches and fry for 8–10 minutes until browned on both sides. Remove with a slotted spoon, drain on kitchen paper, then place on a serving plate.

Fry the mint in batches until just starting to turn. Scatter the courgettes with the finely chopped garlic, chilli and fried mint. Season, drizzle with vinegar and serve at room temperature., topped with burrata.

LEMON & MINT LABNEH BALLS

These make a perfect addition to salads (such as the Cucumber and Herb Grain Salad on page 90) or serve with charred bread as a delicious snack.

150 g/5½ oz. labneh (see page 138)
1 garlic clove, crushed
grated zest of 1 lemon
20 g/¾ oz. fresh mint leaves,
finely chopped

Place the labneh in a bowl with the garlic and lemon zest. Stir together until combined and then roll the flavoured labneh into balls. Place the chopped mint on a plate, then roll the labneh balls in the mint to coat.

Flavour variations

SEED & SPICE Grind 1 teaspoon each coriander seeds and cumin seeds to a powder in a pestle and mortar. Mix with ½ teaspoon ground cinnamon, 1 teaspoon sesame seeds and a pinch of chilli/hot red pepper flakes. Roll plain labneh balls into the spice mix.

PISTACHIO & GREEN OLIVE Mix 100 g/3½ oz. finely chopped pistachios and 50 g/2 oz. finely chopped green olives, then roll plain labneh balls in the mixture.

MARINATED Mix 7 tablespoons extra virgin olive oil with a halved red chilli, 1 sliced lemon and 3 sprigs of fresh rosemary. Place the rolled balls into the oil mixture. Keep refrigerated for up to a week.

RUFFLED RICOTTA & HONEY FILO PIE

A hybrid sweet and savoury pie, this is the type of dish a Greek may eat for breakfast, enjoy as snack when they pop into a friend's house, or serve as part of a feasting table. This recipe features ricotta, but it can be made more savoury by adding tangy feta to the filling, or use more honey and sugar for something on the sweeter side, as you prefer.

7 sheets of filo pastry
85 g/¾ stick unsalted butter, melted, plus extra for greasing
½ teaspoon ground cinnamon

RICOTTA CUSTARD
5 eggs, at room temperature
100 g/3½ oz. runny honey, plus extra for drizzling
100 ml/generous ⅓ cup milk
pinch of sea salt
2 teaspoons pure vanilla paste
200 g/7 oz. ricotta
grated lemon or orange zest (optional)

SERVES 4 TO SHARE

Preheat the oven to 180°C fan/200°/400°F/gas 6. Grease a round 23-cm/9-in. springform pan with melted butter and place the pan on a baking sheet.

Brush each sheet of filo pastry with melted butter and dust the top with cinnamon. Scrunch each filo layer up like an accordion or roll it loosely into a long tube.

Roll the first layer of filo into a spiral and place it in the centre of the prepared pan. Wrap the remaining 6 layers of filo (accordions) around the first spiral.

Brush the top of the pie with the remaining butter and bake on the centre rack in the preheated oven for about 30 minutes until golden.

Meanwhile, make the custard. Put the eggs in a mixing bowl along with half the honey. Put the milk, salt and remaining honey in a saucepan and cook over a medium heat until scalding hot. Whisk the eggs and honey together until frothy. Add the scalding hot milk mixture to the eggs slowly to temper them while whisking constantly. Add the vanilla paste and whisk together. Whisk in the ricotta and citrus zest, if using. Set aside.

As soon as the pan with the filo comes out of the oven, pour the custard on top of it. Return the pan to the oven and bake on the centre rack for another 25 minutes. Once cooked, drizzle with extra honey and an extra sprinkle of sea salt.

WHIPPED SPICY HONEY FETA
with green olives & pea shoots

*Here's a huge flavour punch in just one bowl. Simply serve this
with the quick yogurt pittas (see page 170) for a snack or a side.*

WHIPPED FETA
200 g/7 oz. feta
100 g/3½ oz. ricotta
2 tablespoons Greek yogurt
sea salt and black pepper

SPICY HONEY
2 tablespoons olive oil
1 garlic clove, left whole and
    bruised
3 tablespoons runny honey
2 tablespoons freshly squeezed
    lemon juice
1 teaspoon chilli/hot red pepper
    flakes, plus extra to serve

TO SERVE
20 g/¾ oz. green olives, stoned/
    pitted and chopped
pea shoots and mini cress,
    to garnish
grated lemon zest
Yogurt Pitta (see page 170)

SERVES 4–6 TO SHARE

Place the feta, ricotta and yogurt in a food processor, season with salt and pepper and blend on high for 2–3 minutes until smooth. Taste and add more salt and pepper if needed.

To make the spicy honey, heat the olive oil in a saucepan over a very low heat. Add the bruised garlic and simmer gently. Turn off the heat. Stir in the honey, lemon juice and chilli flakes and season with salt and pepper.

Serve the whipped feta in a bowl, drizzled with the spicy honey and topped with olives, pea shoots and cress, lemon zest and some extra freshly ground black pepper and chilli flakes.

GORGONZOLA & ASPARAGUS FRITTATA

*Traditionally a frittata has a potato base, but this recipe simply uses
in-season asparagus, eggs, herbs and spring onions/scallions, finished
with gorgonzola. Perfect for a light summer supper with a glass of rosé.
If asparagus is out of season, courgettes/zucchini are a great alternative.*

small knob of butter

1 shallot, finely chopped

4 spring onions/scallions,
    finely chopped

200 g/7 oz. asparagus,
    woody ends snapped off

6 eggs, beaten

grated zest of 1 lemon

100 g/3½ oz. gorgonzola,
    crumbled

salad leaves, to serve

sea salt and black pepper

SERVES 2

Heat the butter in a small frying pan/skillet over a low heat. Add the shallot and spring onions and cook gently for 8 minutes until soft and translucent, stirring to stop them catching. Add the asparagus and cook for 3 minutes, stirring.

Preheat the grill/broiler.

Pour the eggs into the pan, sprinkle over the lemon zest and season with salt and pepper. Cook until almost set, without stirring. Sprinkle over the cheese and pop under the grill/broiler until just set and the cheese is melted and golden. Leave to cool slightly and serve warm, cut into wedges, with a green salad.

Variations

ROASTED RED PEPPER, SPINACH & FETA Drain and slice a 400-g/14-oz. jar of roasted red peppers. In a frying pan/skillet, sauté 1 finely chopped shallot in a little of the oil from the jar, add the peppers and 200 g/7 oz. sliced baby spinach and allow to wilt. Mix through 6 beaten eggs and cook until set. Crumble 200 g/5 oz. feta over the top, allow to melt, then sprinkle over a pinch of chilli/red hot pepper flakes.

NEW POTATO, TOMATO & MANCHEGO Cook 300 g/10 ½ oz. new potatoes, then slice. In a frying pan/skillet sauté 1 finely chopped shallot in a little oil until soft, add the sliced potatoes and 100 g/3½ oz. semi-dried tomatoes and cook for 5 minutes. Add 50 g/2 oz. grated Manchego, 20 g/1 oz. freshly chopped parsley, zest of 1 lemon and stir through 6 beaten eggs. Cook until firm and golden.

yogurt, labneh & feta

Yogurt

Yogurt is a dairy product made by fermenting milk with a yogurt culture. It provides protein and calcium, and it may enhance healthy gut bacteria.

The first traces of yogurt have been discovered to date back to between 10,000 and 5,000 BCE, in the Neolithic period – a time when nomadic people were turning themselves to a new way of life of domestication and the beginnings of agriculture. At that time, humans were starting to domesticate animals such as cows, goats, buffalo, yaks and camels, which produced milk.

Before anything was known about bacteria, lactose in milk was converted to lactic acid thanks to starter cultures, thus prevent milk from pathogens. This transformation came about by mixing fresh milk with small amounts of sour milk. For people living in precarious conditions, fermented dairy products were a safe way to preserve milk. In the early 1900s the first yogurt factory was introduced in France to mass-produce yogurt. Before that it was made locally. What we know as traditional Greek yogurt is made by straining normal yogurt to achieve a thicker texture.

Labneh

Labneh is made from Greek yogurt and it is strained further which then makes it a yogurt cheese. While Greek yogurt has a creamy texture, labneh is a little more like soft cheese in texture. This makes it easy to roll into balls, encase in herbs, drizzle with olive oil. It has a thick texture, similar to that of cream cheese, and a tanginess that lands somewhere between cream cheese and yogurt. Though made it's mostly made by using Greek yogurt, it was traditionally made with goat's milk and strained for longer, helping it to achieve that thick, spreadable consistency ideal for spreading with a spoon and creating swirls in which olive oil can pool.

Feta

Feta is a soft cheese made from whole sheep's milk or a combination of sheep's milk and goat's milk. In Greece, feta is cured in a salty brine. Known as a pickled cheese, its flavour becomes sharper and saltier with age and the cheese becomes more firm. Feta is creamy white in colour, with small holes and a crumbly texture. It normally comes in square cakes with no rind, but you can also find pre-crumbled feta packaged in airtight containers without brine and with or without added seasonings. It costs more than other common cheeses, but a little goes a long way.

FETA & GRIDDLED WATERMELON PLATE
with pink peppercorn & Aleppo chilli-infused olive oil & green olives

In this salad the feta has been softened to make it creamy and the watermelon has been griddled to give a charred flavour and to caramelize the sugars, truly transforming simple ingredients into something far more exciting.

1 tablespoon olive oil

1 mini watermelon, cut into thick slices

2 avocados, peeled, stoned/pitted and sliced

100 g/3½ oz. green olives, stoned/pitted

100 g/3½ oz. feta cheese

10 g/⅓ oz. fresh mint leaves

1 tablespoon runny honey

juice of ½ lemon (or to taste)

2–3 tablespoons pink pepper and Aleppo chilli-infused olive oil (see below)

100 g/3½ oz. rocket/arugula (optional)

sea salt and black pepper

INFUSED OIL

100 ml/3½ oz. extra virgin olive oil

½ tablespoon pink peppercorns, crushed

1 tablespoon Aleppo chilli/hot red pepper flakes

SERVES 4

At least 1 hour before serving, infuse the olive oil by placing all the ingredients in a saucepan and gently bring to heat. Take care not to boil or burn the oil. Leave to cool and store in a clean glass jar or bottle (see page 4) until needed.

For the salad, brush a griddle pan with oil and set over a medium heat. Add the watermelon to the pan and cook for 2–3 minutes each side until charred on both sides. The idea is to create a charred flavour and caramelize the sugars in the fruit, not to cook it, so it is best to have the griddle pan piping hot.

On a platter, place the watermelon slices, top with the avocado, green olives, feta, mint, honey and lemon juice. Drizzle with the infused oil and season. For an extra touch of green, add some rocket/arugula, if liked.

BUTTERNUT & RICOTTA GNOCCHI
with walnuts & sage

Sometimes you want to eat something that is lighter than potato gnocchi but just as comforting. This dish hits the mark with the addition of ricotta, making a sweet, earthy and creamy gnocchi dish.

1 butternut squash, peeled, deseeded and chopped into chunks

1 egg, beaten

250-g/9-oz. tub of ricotta

150 g/generous 1 cup plain/all-purpose flour

½ teaspoon freshly grated nutmeg

20 g/¾ oz. Parmesan, grated, plus extra to serve

45 g/3 tablespoons butter

2 tablespoons olive oil

handful of fresh sage

30 g/1 oz. walnuts, chopped

sea salt and black pepper

SERVES 2

Place the squash in a saucepan of boiling water and cook for 15 minutes, then drain well. Transfer to a bowl and mash with a masher or fork. Tip into a sieve or colander and press with a spoon to squeeze out as much water as possible.

Place the mashed squash in a bowl. Add the beaten egg, along with the ricotta, flour, nutmeg and Parmesan. Season with plenty of salt and pepper and stir to mix. You should have a thick, slightly sticky mixture – not quite a dough but close to it. Set aside.

Bring a large saucepan of water to the boil. Scoop 1 tablespoon out of the gnocchi mix. Scoop between two spoons to shape into an oval and drop into the water. Repeat until you have 6–8 gnocchi in the pan. Simmer for 2–4 minutes until they float – the water will go cloudy.

Lift the gnocchi out of the pan with a slotted spoon and repeat with the rest of the mix.

Melt half the butter with a splash of oil in a frying pan/skillet over a medium heat. Add the gnocchi and fry for 5–8 minutes until golden, turning once or twice.

Melt the rest of the butter in the pan. Pick the sage leaves off the stalks and add them to the pan with the walnuts . Fry for 1 minute until they sizzle, then spoon over the gnocchi. Serve with extra Parmesan.

RATATOUILLE TART
with mascarpone, mozzarella & basil

A perfect tart to serve to friends. It can be eaten warm or at room temperature, so can sit until you are ready to eat. This goes well alongside a charcuterie board and a crisp salad. Best eaten on the day of making.

2 courgettes /zucchini,
    cut into 5-mm/¼-in. slices
1 aubergine/eggplant,
    cut into 5-mm/¼-in. slices
3 tablespoons olive oil,
    plus extra for drizzling
3 large tomatoes (a mixture of
    different colours looks nice),
    cut into 5-mm/¼-in. slices
1 x 320-g/11½-oz. sheet of
    ready-rolled puff pastry
4 tablespoons mascarpone
2 mozzarella balls, sliced
1 egg, beaten to glaze
fresh basil leaves, to garnish
100 g/3½ oz. roasted red (bell)
    peppers from a jar, sliced
sea salt and black pepper

SERVES 4–6

Preheat the oven to 220°C fan/240°C/475°F/gas 9.

Lay the courgette and aubergine slices out on a couple of large baking sheets and brush them on both sides with 2 tablespoons of the olive oil. Season, roast in the preheated oven for 10 minutes until starting to soften, then leave to cool for 10 minutes. Meanwhile, pat the tomato slices dry and leave to drain on paper towels.

Put a large baking sheet on the top shelf of the oven to heat up. Unroll the puff pastry sheet on a floured work surface and roll out further in one direction to make a square about 3-mm/⅛-in. thick, then trim off the corners to make a 30-cm/12-in. round disc. Transfer the pastry circle to a large piece of non-stick baking paper so that it's easier to move once it's assembled.

Spread the marsacapone over the centre of the pastry, leaving a 5-cm/2-in. border all round the edge and season with salt and pepper. Layer up slices of courgette, aubergine, tomato, red peppers and mozzarella and arrange on top of the mascarpone in a spiral or concentric circles.

Drizzle with another tablespoon of oil and fold in the sides to overlap the filling slightly, making a 3–4 cm/1½–1¾ in. wide crust. Brush the crust with egg, sprinkle with a little salt and slide the tart, on its paper, onto the hot baking skeet in the oven.

Bake for 20–25 minutes until the pastry is puffed and golden and the vegetables have softened. Leave to rest for at least 20 minutes.

Serve warm or at room temperature, scattered with basil and drizzled with more oil.

FRESH FIG, WHIPPED GOAT'S CHEESE, RICOTTA & ROCKET *on a thin & crispy pizza base*

A thin and crispy pizza base, topped with creamy goat's cheese, juicy syrupy figs and blackberries. The blackberries add a juicy, sweet tartness but any soft berry can be used here, whatever is in season. It is equally delicious if you only have figs.

BASE

5 g/1 teaspoon dried yeast

50 ml/3½ tablespoons lukewarm water

350 g/2½ cups strong white bread flour, plus extra for dusting

1 tablespoon sea salt

60 ml/¼ cup extra-virgin olive oil, plus extra for drizzling

TOPPING

100 g/3½ oz. soft goat's cheese

100 g/3½ oz. ricotta

6 fresh figs, cut into 5-mm/ ¼-in. slices

50 g/2 oz. blackberries (optional)

2 handfuls of rocket/arugula

2 tablespoons olive oil

1 tablespoon balsamic vinegar

1 tablespoon runny honey

sea salt and black pepper

MAKES 3 PIZZAS

Combine the yeast and lukewarm water in a small bowl, stir to dissolve and set aside until foamy. Combine the flour, salt and olive oil in an electric mixer fitted with a dough hook. Add the yeast mixture and 150 ml/⅔ cup water and knead until well combined. Stand at room temperature, covered with a damp tea/dish towel for about 1 hour, or until doubled in size.

Preheat the oven to 220°C fan/240°C/475°F/gas 9 or the highest setting.

To make the topping in a stand mixer, whip the soft goat's cheese with the ricotta and season well.

Turn the dough onto a bench and knock back, dusting lightly with flour, and bring mixture just together to form a smooth soft dough. Divide into 3 balls, then place on a lightly floured surface and cover with a lightly floured tea/dish towel for about 20 minutes until doubled in size.

Put one of the balls of dough on a flour-dusted 22-cm/9-in. diameter pizza tray and press outwards from the centre to flatten and stretch into a circle. Repeat with the other balls of dough. Drizzle with olive oil and bake in the preheated oven for 8 minutes.

Remove from the oven and spread the surface with the whipped cheese and top with the figs and blackberries, if using. Return to the oven for another 5–7 minutes. Take out of the oven and top with the rocket and drizzle with olive oil, balsamic vinegar and honey.

ex lardario
FROM THE LARDER
Sauces, condiments & pickles

SIMPLE SUMMER TOMATO SAUCE

There is nothing more satisfying than making your own tomato sauce. This sauce combines the velvety base of bought passata/strained tomatoes, adding in cherry tomatoes as well as other flavour enhancers. The addition of the cherry tomatoes makes it a perfect simple summer tomato sauce that can be used in so many dishes.

100 ml/generous ⅓ cup extra virgin olive oil
1 onion, finely chopped
3 garlic cloves, crushed
500 g/1 lb. 2 oz. cherry tomatoes, halved
800 ml/3⅓ cups passata/strained tomatoes
1 teaspoon dried oregano
pinch of sugar
30 g/1 oz. fresh basil leaves, torn
sea salt and black pepper

MAKES 2–3 JARS

Stir the oil, onion and garlic together in a large saucepan over a low heat until golden. Add the tomatoes, season to taste and continue to cook, stirring occasionally, until falling apart. Add the passata, oregano and sugar and simmer for about 30 minutes until thickened. Remove from the heat and stir in the basil. Decant into sterilized jars (see page 4).

The sauce will keep in the refrigerator for 1 week. Alternatively, freeze in batches and you will have a lovely fresh tomato sauce to hand whenever you need it.

PARSLEY OIL

For that extra drizzle of something vibrant to any dish, be it over burrata, finishing pasta or over a pizza, then this parsley oil adds an extra dimension. The oil can be used in a vinaigrette, in cold soups or to garnish chicken or fish.

100 g/3½ oz. fresh flat-leaf parsley
3 garlic cloves, coarsely chopped
125 ml/½ cup extra virgin olive oil

MAKES 1 SMALL JAR

Put the parsley and garlic in a food processor or blender and blend until coarsely chopped. With the motor running, gradually add the oil and process until very smooth. Transfer to a muslin-lined sieve placed over a bowl and set aside until all parsley oil has drained through. Discard the solids and decant the oil into a sterilized bottle (see page 4). It will keep in the fridge for 1 week.

PICKLES

Pickling is the process of preserving or extending the shelf life. The pickling procedure typically affects the food's texture and flavour. It can be a quick pickle that is eaten on the day, or a week pickle or a longterm pickle.
Pictured on pages 154–155

GIARDINIERA
Italian garden pickle

Giardiniera is a versatile mix of pickled vegetables that is served as part of an antipasto spread. Making the most of crunchy, colourful vegetables that remind you of a spring garden, it is a refreshing side to a sharing board of charcuterie and cheeses.

1 litre/4 cups white wine vinegar
3 bay leaves
1 teaspoon whole cloves
1 teaspoon black peppercorns
1 tablespoon sea salt
1 medium head of cauliflower,
    cut into small florets
250 g/9 oz. carrots, cut into
    battons
250 g/9 oz. celery, cut into chunks

*500-g/18-oz. sterilized jars
    (see page 4)*

MAKES 2–3 JARS

Pour the vinegar into a large, non-reactive pan set over a high heat and add the bay leaves, cloves, peppercorns and salt and bring to the boil. Add the cauliflower, carrots and celery. Lower the heat and simmer for about 15 minutes.

Using a slotted spoon, transfer the cooked vegetables to the sterilized jars and top up with the hot vinegar. (Have more boiling hot vinegar handy in case you need more to top off the jars.)

Seal the filled jars tightly and leave them to cool. Store them in the fridge for up to 1 month – the longer they sit, the more robust the flavour will become.

PICKLED CABBAGE
Greek mountain style

Although this is pickled in winter, it is eaten all year around, it pairs beautifully with simple soups and bread. Try it shredded onto a sandwich or with a hunk of cheese. One of life's simple pleasures.

1 head white cabbage,
  leaves stripped

100 g/3½ oz. sea salt

3–4 garlic cloves, peeled

1 onion, sliced

1 litre/4 cups white wine vinegar

150 g/¾ cup caster/granulated
  sugar

1 teaspoon cloves

1 tesapoon black peppercorns

glass/plastic containers

MAKES 1.5 LITRES/3 LB.

Rinse the cabbage and place in a large bowl, sprinkle with the salt and mix so all the cabbage is well coated. Cover and leave overnight. The next day, pack the containers tightly with cabbage and the garlic and onion. Add in the cloves and peppercorns.

Mix the vinegar, sugar and 500 ml/2 cups water together in a jug/pitcher, then pour into the jar so that the vegetables are well covered. Leave to pickle for a week before using.

QUICK PICKLED CUCUMBER

A crisp cucumber's mellow flavour makes it ideal for pickling, and it's a refreshing addition to a chilled soup during the summer. Try a slice in gin cocktails, too.

2 cucumbers, finely sliced

2 teaspoons sea salt

1½ tablespoons white wine vinegar

1½ tablespoons caster/superfine
  sugar

handful of fresh dill, chopped
  (optional)

SERVES 4 TO SHARE

Toss the cucumbers with the salt and tip into a colander. Cover with a saucer and place a weight, such as a can of beans, on top. Set aside for about 20 minutes.

Remove the plate and squeeze the cucumber gently between your hands to get rid of any excess water, then pat dry with paper towels. Toss with the vinegar and sugar and a handful of chopped dill, if liked. Serve within 30 minutes (this needs to be eaten fresh).

BAY & JUNIPER-PICKLED GRAPES

This is one type of pickle you can have a play with. Every variety of grape imparts a different flavour. On the second day of pickling and as the grapes start to ferment, they leave a bubbling sensation as you eat them.

200 ml/¾–1 cup white wine vinegar

50 ml/3½ tablespoons red wine vinegar

50 g/¼ cup caster/superfine sugar

50 g/3 tablespoons runny honey

10 juniper berries

3 bay leaves

500 g/1 lb. 2 oz. red seedless grapes

MAKES A 600-ML/21-OZ. JAR

Bring the vinegars, sugar, honey, juniper berries and bay leaves to a simmer in a saucepan over a high heat for about 5 minutes, stirring to dissolve the sugar. Put the grapes in a sterilized 600-ml/21-oz. jar (see page 4), pour over the hot pickling liquid, seal and leave to cool to room temperature, then refrigerate for 4 hours or overnight.

Serve with a selection of cheeses, dried figs and foccacia. Pickled grapes are best eaten within a week (store in the fridge).

WHOLE PICKLED SUMAC SHALLOTS

Add these to salads, serve with cheese, as part of an antipasti platter, with mezze... If you are a pickle lover you can have these with almost anything. Pickled shallots are more mellow and just a little sweeter than onions and surprisingly delicate.

200 ml/¾–1 cup good-quality white wine vinegar

100 g/½ cup caster/superfine sugar

1 tablespoon sea salt

6 cardamom pods, bruised

300 g/10½ oz. small shallots, peeled

1 tablespoon sumac

1 tablespoon mustard seeds

MAKES A 1-LITRE/35-OZ. JAR

Bring the vinegar, sugar, salt and cardamom to the boil in a small saucepan over a medium heat, stirring until the sugar and salt have dissolved. Add the shallots and return the liquid to the boil. Add the sumac and mustard seeds, then transfer the shallots and hot liquid to a heatproof bowl or jar.

Leave to cool, then transfer to a sterilized jar (see page 4). Allow to stand for 3 days before eating (if you can wait that long!).

MAYONNAISE & AÏOLI

Mayonnaise is made by emulsifying eggs, oil, and some type of acid, usually vinegar or lemon juice (emulsification means combining two or more liquids that normally are unmixable). Although aïoli and mayonnaise are both creamy emulsions, aïoli is made from garlic and olive oil while mayo is made from egg yolks and a light olive oil. The final result may look similar but the two sauces have distinctly different flavours.
Pictured on pages 160–161

BASIC MAYONNAISE

2 egg yolks
1 tablespoon Dijon mustard
350 ml/1½ cups light olive oil
2 teaspoons freshly squeezed
    lemon juice
sea salt and black pepper

SERVES 4 AS A CONDIMENT

Mix the egg yolks and mustard together in a bowl until completely combined, then season with salt and pepper. Whisking constantly, add a small drop of oil and whisk until completely combined, then add another drop and continue a drop at a time until the yolks and oil combine and start to thicken. Once you are confident the oil and eggs are coming together you can add the oil a bit more at a time, but be patient, as adding the oil too quickly will cause the mayonnaise to split and curdle.

Once all the oil has been whisked into the eggs and you have a thick, spoonable mayonnaise, whisk in the lemon juice and season to taste or add other flavourings. Keeps in the fridge for 2 days.

Mayonnaise flavour variations

PRESERVED LEMON & PARSLEY Add 1-2 finely chopped preserved lemons and 20 g/1 oz. finely chopped parsley to 1 quantity of mayonnaise, mix well and serve as an accompaniment to barbecued fish.

HARISSA & THYME Mix 1–2 tablespoons harissa paste and the leaves from 2–3 sprigs of fresh thyme with 1 quantity of mayonnaise for the perfect accompaniment to pork kebabs.

WATERCRESS & CAPER Blitz 50 g/2 oz. watercress with 2 tablespoons chopped capers and a squeeze of lemon juice and mix with 1 quantity of mayonnaise for a vibrant green topping in a fish burger or a lovely side for roasted vegetables.

TARRAGON & MUSTARD Mix the chopped leaves from 3 sprigs of fresh tarragon, 1 teaspoon Dijon mustard and 1 teaspoon wholegrain mustard with 1 quantity of mayonnaise and serve with ham, pickles and freshly baked still-warm bread.

VEGAN MAYONNAISE

60 ml/¼ cup aquafaba
   (brine from a can of chickpeas)
1 teaspoon Dijon mustard
1 teaspoon sea salt
2 teaspoons apple cider vinegar
2 teaspoons maple syrup
180–240 ml/¾–1 cup sunflower oil
black pepper

SERVES 4 AS A CONDIMENT

Put the aquafaba in a food processor with the mustard, salt, vinegar and maple syrup and pulse until all blended well.

With the food processor on, slowly stream the oil in over the course of 1–2 minutes. This will allow the mixture to emulsify and gently thicken. If it's looking too thin, add more oil. The more oil you add, the creamier, thicker and denser the texture will become. You shouldn't need more than the recommended amount. Taste and adjust the flavour by adding acid or sweetness, salt and pepper.

Use immediately or transfer to a sealed container in the fridge for about 4 hours until cold. It will thicken even more in the fridge. Keeps in the fridge for 2 days.

SAFFRON AÏOLI

pinch of saffron threads
1 tablespoon boiling water
2 egg yolks
1 small garlic clove, crushed
1 tablespoon Dijon mustard
freshly squeezed juice of ½ lemon
200 ml/¾–1 cup olive oil
black pepper

SERVES 4 AS A CONDIMENT

Put the saffron in a small bowl with the boiling water. Leave for 10 minutes to cool and for the water to turn a golden colour.

Meanwhile, put the egg yolks, garlic, mustard and lemon juice in a food processor and pulse until smooth. Slowly add the olive oil, a small drizzle at a time, keeping the machine on, until you get a thick, glossy mayonnaise. Season with black pepper, then stir in the saffron water to loosen the aïoli and turn it a golden hue. Cover the surface and chill until ready to serve. Add a splash of water or lemon juice, to serve, if your aïoli thickens up too much in the fridge. Keeps in the fridge for 2 days.

vinegar

Vinegar is a larder staple. It can be used in sauces, marinades, dressings and for pickling. It is an acidic, subtly sour-tasting component that punches up dishes and serves as a balancing component in sauces and marinades. The word 'vinegar' comes from the Latin for 'sour wine'. Essentially, it is fermented juice that has turned sour due to the growth of naturally-occurring bacteria. Vinegar comes in a huge variety of flavours, so it does not always taste sour.

Its origins date back over 3,000 years to Ancient Babylon, where it was considered the poor person's wine. However, vinegar is the most useful condiment. In addition to serving as a form of alcohol, ancients also used the liquid to enhance the flavours of their cooking and to preserve and pickle foods. There is a huge array of vinegars but the list below features those most often used in Mediterranean cuisine (other types, such as rice, malt and black vinegar are used in Asian cookery).

DISTILLED WHITE VINEGAR Made by distilling vinegar with steam heat, which kills all nutrients and essentially boils the liquid down to pure acetic acid. For this reason, you really do not want to use distilled white vinegar for most cooking tasks. That said, it is the most common choice for pickling because it is high in acetic acid yet it will not change the colour of your food. Great for pickling, poaching eggs, baking.

BALSAMIC VINEGAR A staple in Italian cuisine, it's made from pressed grape juice rather than fermented alcohol, which gives it a more mellow and fruity flavour profile. The dark red liquid is traditionally made from grapes, but it may be mixed with other fruits to give it a deeper or more complex flavour. It is beloved for its sweet taste and concentrated, syrup-like concentration. Great for dressings, glazes, drizzles, dips, marinades, reductions.

WHITE WINE VINEGAR Made when white wine is fermented and oxidized into an acid and then distilled. White wine vinegar tends to have a mild flavour profile that is subtly fruity. This makes it for cooking and brining. Unlike red wine vinegar, white wine vinegar will not stain your foods, so it is a good choice for brining and pickling. It is also a staple in many classic sauces, including hollandaise, béarnaise and a good vinaigrette. Great for brining, condiments, pickling, dressings, sauces, drizzles, soups, stews, fillings, marinades.

RED WINE VINEGAR Similar to white wine vinegar in that it is made from the grapes of said wine through a process of fermentation and distillation. Use when you do not mind a little red stain (such as pickled turnips or red onions). It is also used in mignonette, the classic sauce drizzled atop fresh oysters. Great for dressings, sauces, pickling, marinades.

CHAMPAGNE VINEGAR Crafted from white grapes and may feature other fruits as well for a deeper flavour profile. This vinegar tends to be milder and more delicate in flavour than other vinegars, which makes it perfect in elegant dressings and marinades. Great for dressings, marinades, sauces, drizzles, cocktails.

SHERRY VINEGAR A Spanish and Basque staple made by fermenting fortified wine in oak barrels. This gives it a well-rounded, complex flavour profile. Although not as popular as balsamic vinegar, sherry vinegar has gained quite the following among devoted chefs. It is more delicate and medium-bodied, so keep this in mind when devising dishes. Great for dressings, glazes, drizzles, dips, marinades, reductions.

APPLE CIDER VINEGAR Made by fermenting sugar from apples, which turns them into acetic acid, creating a punchy flavour that is fruity and tart. Studies show it is also helpful for weight loss and skin health. Useful when making marinades, dressings, sauces and more that require a tart taste. Great for pickling, marinades, sauces.

SALAD DRESSINGS

A good dressing is a sauce for salads, and here is a selection of three dressings you will make time and time again. Ideal for virtually all leafy salads, dressings may also be used when making salads of beans, noodle or pasta and antipasti, and forms of potato salad.

HERB VINAIGRETTE

2 spring onions/scallions, chopped
1 garlic clove
3 tablespoons apple cider vinegar
2 tablespoons freshly squeezed lemon (or lime) juice
large handful of mixed fresh herbs (parsley, basil and a little thyme and mint)
60 ml/¼ cup olive oil
¼ teaspoon cayenne pepper
½ teaspoon sea salt
¼ teaspoon black pepper

MAKES ENOUGH FOR 1 SALAD

Put the spring onions, garlic, apple cider vinegar, lemon juice, herbs, olive oil, cayenne, salt and pepper in a food processor and blend until smooth. Store in the fridge until ready to use (best used fresh).

SERVE WITH classic salad leaves, such as cos lettuce, lollo rosso, spinach and thinly sliced radishes.

LEMON & OREGANO

freshly squeezed juice of 2 lemons
1 teaspoon dried oregano
1 garlic clove, crushed
pinch of sea salt
1 teaspoon freshly ground black pepper
1 teaspoon Dijon mustard (optional)
squeeze of runny honey (optional or to taste)
200 ml/¾–1 cup extra virgin olive oil

MAKES ENOUGH FOR 1 SALAD

Whisk together the lemon juice, oregano, garlic, salt and pepper and mustard and honey, if using, in a medium bowl. Continue whisking while adding the oil in slow, steady stream. Cover and refrigerate until ready to use (best used fresh).

SERVE WITH roughly chopped beef tomatoes, chopped cucumber, crumbled feta, sliced red onions and fresh parsley.

ORANGE & HAZELNUT

grated zest and juice of 1 orange
100 ml/generous ⅓ cup hazelnut oil
1 teaspoon Dijon mustard
sea salt and black pepper
30 g/1 oz. chopped hazelnuts (optional)

MAKES ENOUGH FOR 1 SALAD

Whisk all the ingredients together in a bowl or jar (best used fresh).

SERVE drizzled over burrata with orange segments, endive and sourdough croutons.

GREEN OLIVE TAPENADE

Tapenade is a Provençal name for a spread or condiment consisting of puréed or finely chopped olives, capers and anchovies. It traditionally, uses black olives but there are many variations using green olives, dried tomatoes and herbs. It can be a dressing, used to top a pasta dish, spread onto a crostini or served alongside a charcuterie board.

300 g/10½ oz. stoned/pitted
    green olives
6 anchovy fillets (or to taste)
100 g/½ cup pine nuts
30 g/½ cup fresh basil
30 g/½ cup fresh parsley
30 g/¼ cup capers, drained
1 garlic clove, crushed
grated zest of 1 lemon
1 teaspoon Kosher salt
120 ml/½ cup extra virgin olive oil

SERVES 4 TO SHARE

Combine the olives, anchovies, pine nuts, basil, parsley, capers, garlic and lemon zest in a food processor fitted with the blade attachment. Pulse until coarsely chopped.

Add the salt and olive oil, then blend into a smooth paste. Taste and adjust the seasoning, adding more salt as needed.

Use immediately or store in an airtight container in the fridge until needed (use within 1 week), allowing to sit at room temperature for 30 minutes before serving. Drizzle with a little extra olive oil and pine nuts, if desired.

BLACK OLIVE TAPENADE

300 g/10½ oz. stoned/pitted
    kalamata olives
1 tablespoon capers
2 anchovy fillets
60 ml/¼ cup extra virgin olive oil
grated zest and juice of 1 lemon
1 teaspoon runny honey (optional)
pinch of chilli (hot red pepper)
    flakes (optional)
3 thyme sprigs (leaves picked)
freshly ground black pepper

SERVES 4 TO SHARE

Blitz all the ingredients except the thyme in a small food processor. Season with black pepper. Use immediately or store in an airtight container in the fridge until needed (use within 3 days).

Allow to sit at room temperature for 30 minutes before serving. Drizzle with extra olive oil and sprinkle with the thyme leaves.

PESTOS

Traditional pesto is a thick, green sauce that tastes bright and herby due to the basil, and salty and rich from the cheeses and pine nuts. It should be garlicky, with pleasant grassiness from good-quality olive oil. The variation using pecorino, sun-dried tomatoes and walnuts is a nice twist. Or for something more modern, try the pistachio and feta version.

CLASSIC PINE NUT & BASIL

50 g/1¾ oz. toasted pine nuts
100 g/3½ oz. fresh basil leaves
100 g/1⅓ cups grated Parmesan
2 garlic cloves
200 ml/¾–1 cup extra virgin
   olive oil
sea salt and black pepper

MAKES 300 G/1½ CUPS

Put all the ingredients in a food processor and whizz until smooth, then season to taste. Store in the fridge for up to 3 days, covered with oil and clingfilm/plastic wrap.

SERVE WITH SPAGHETTI GENOVESE
Simply cook 300 g/10½ oz. sliced new potatoes, 300 g/10½ oz. spaghetti and 200 g/7 oz. green beans cut in half, then mix with 120 g/4½ oz. of this fresh pesto with some extra basil leaves.

WALNUT & SUN-DRIED TOMATO

100 g/3½ oz. pecorino, grated
120 g/4½ oz. sun-dried tomatoes
bunch of fresh basil
100 g/3½ oz. walnuts
1 garlic clove
2 tablespoons sun-dried tomato oil
50 ml/3½ tablespoons extra virgin
   olive oil
sea salt and black pepper

MAKES 300 G/1½ CUPS

Put all the ingredients in a food processor and whizz until smooth, then season to taste. Store in the fridge for up to 3 days, covered with oil and clingfilm/plastic wrap.

SERVE WITH SUN-DRIED TOMATO, CHEESE, WALNUT, RED CHILLI & BASIL FLAT BREAD
Simply spread 100 g/3½ oz. of this pesto onto 2 flatbreads, then top with cheese, walnuts, red chilli/chile, drizzle with olive oil and bake for 12–15 minutes in an oven preheated to 180°C fan/200°C/400°F/gas 6. Serve topped with fresh basil.

PISTACHIO & FETA

½ bunch of fresh basil
½ bunch of fresh mint, leaves
   picked
185 ml/¾ cup extra virgin olive oil
100 g/3½ oz. pistachio nuts,
   plus extra, crushed, to serve
2 small garlic cloves
3 tablespoons finely grated
   Parmesan
grated zest of 1 lemon
50 g/1¾ oz. feta cheese, crumbled

MAKES 300 G/1½ CUPS

Put the basil, mint, olive oil, garlic and Parmesan in a food processor and blitz. Finish with lemon zest and feta. Store in the fridge for up to 3 days, covered with oil and clingfilm/plastic wrap.

SERVE WITH COURGETTE SALAD
Put 2 thinly sliced courgettes/zucchini in a bowl with 200 g/7 oz. halved cherry tomatoes, 1 thinly sliced red onion, 2 handfuls of rocket/arugula, fresh mint leaves and gently mix the pesto through. Top with extra pistachios and serve with crusty bread.

ab igne

FROM THE FIRE

Breads

HOME-MADE YOGURT PITTA

These super quick and easy yogurt flatbreads are made with a combination of simple ingredients. Light and fluffy flatbreads are great for serving with dips, curries, soups and stews.

7-g/¼-oz. sachet of fast-action
   dry yeast
200 ml/¾–1 cup warm water
450 g/3¼ cups strong bread flour
1 teaspoon sea salt
3 tablespoons extra virgin olive oil,
   plus extra for greasing
200 g/7 oz. Greek yogurt

***MAKES 8–10 SMALL–MEDIUM
PITTAS OR 5–6 LARGE ONES***

Mix the yeast in the water (making sure the water is not too hot).

Combine the flour and salt in a stand mixer with the dough hook attachment. Add the yeast mixture, oil and yogurt and mix to combine. Knead the dough, adding more flour if needed, for about 7–10 minutes until it's soft and slightly sticky. Transfer the dough to an oiled bowl, cover with a clean tea/dish towel, and leave to rise for about 2 hours until it has doubled in size.

Preheat the oven to 200°C fan/220°C/425°F/gas 7. Line a baking sheet with non-stick baking paper.

Turn the dough out onto a clean work surface and divide it into equal balls (the number depends on the size of pittas you are making). Cover and leave to rise for another 20 minutes.

Roll the dough balls out into circles that are 1 cm/½ in. thick. Place a few on the lined baking sheet with space between them. Bake in batches until they're puffy and lightly browned on top. Begin checking at 5 minutes, rotating the baking sheet if one side of the pittas is puffing up more than the other. Cook for another 3 minutes. Transfer the pittas to a wire rack to cool.

POTATO & ROSEMARY FOCCACIA

You'll need to start this foccacia 12–18 hours before baking it, but once you use this method you will never go back. It's super bubbly and tasty, and the flavour develops as it slowly proves in the fridge. Once you remove it from the fridge, leave it untouched until it comes to room temperature. Then you are ready to go and top it with what you like – thinly sliced new potatoes work beautifully.

500 g/3½–3⅔ cups strong
    bread flour
2 teaspoons sea salt
8 g/¼ oz. instant yeast
5 tablespoons olive oil, plus extra
    for greasing
3 fresh rosemary sprigs,
    leaves picked
200 g/7 oz. new potatoes,
    thinly sliced
2 fresh thyme sprigs, leaves picked

MAKES 1 FOCCACIA LOAF

Start this recipe 12–18 hours before needed.

Mix the flour, salt and yeast well in a bowl. Add 450 ml/1¾ cups water, then mix well with a spatula to form a dough. Leave the dough in the bowl, slick it with olive oil and cover with clingfilm/plastic wrap – this is important to prevent it drying out in the fridge.

Place the bowl in the fridge immediately; leave it there to rise for 12–18 hours or up to 3 days. When ready to use, remove from the fridge, knock back and put in a 20 x 30-cm/8 x 12-in. pan greased with olive oil.

Don't touch the dough again for 2–4 hours to allow it to come to room temperature slowly (this will depend on how warm your kitchen environment is). It is ready when if feels just warm to the touch, has doubled in size and is nice and 'bubbly'.

Preheat the oven to 180°C fan/200°C/400°F/gas 6.

Pour 2 tablespoons of the olive oil over the dough, and using your fingers, press straight down to create deep dimples. Sprinkle with flaky sea salt, the sliced potatoes and herbs. Or simply dimple, drizzle with oil and sea salt and bake.

Transfer to the preheated oven immediately and bake for 25 minutes, or until golden all over. Remove the focaccia from the pan and place on a cooling rack to cool completely.

OVERNIGHT FLATBREAD THREE WAYS

Make this dough the night before and let it sit in the fridge to ramp up the flavour. As well as a simple flatbread that can be eaten on its own or added to a flatbread salad, try these mini harissa flatbreads topped with courgette flowers and the large nigella and crispy onion version.
Pictured on pages 176–177

BASIC FLATBREADS

650 ml/2¾ cups water, at room
   temperature
7-g/¼-oz. sachet of fast-action
   dry yeast
50 g/3½ tablespoons sunflower oil
1 kg/7–7¼ cups bread flour
20 g/4 teaspoons sea salt

**MAKES 2 LARGE OR 4 SMALL
FLATBREADS**

The night before, pour the water into a large bowl, whisk in the yeast, then stir in the oil. Add the flour and salt, combine to a shaggy mixture, then leave covered for an hour. Knead the dough lightly for about 2 minutes, then return it to the bowl and cover with clingfilm/plastic wrap. Place in the fridge for a day or so (I find it's fine for up to 3 days when kept chilled).

Preheat the oven to 220°C fan/240°C/475°F/gas 9.

Divide the dough into 2 or 4 equal portions. Flour your hands to prevent them sticking to the mixture, then press and pull the dough into an oval. Dust each piece lightly with flour, then stack each on a plate, separating them with a sheet of lightly oiled parchment paper. Remove the dough and brush both sides lightly with olive oil. Add toppings (see recipes below and right). Arrange the flatbread on a lightly oiled baking sheet and bake for 7–10 minutes or until the bottoms are golden. Turn and continue cooking for another 3–4 minutes.

LARGE FLATBREAD *with onion & nigella seeds*

½ quantity of Basic Flatbread
   (see above), brought to room
   temperature
flour, for dusting
1 teaspoon nigella seeds
1 teaspoon crispy onion flakes
2 tablespoons olive oil
sea salt and black pepper
super ripe tomatoes, olive oil,
   onions and olives, to serve

MAKES 1 LARGE FLATBREAD

Preheat the oven to 220°C fan/240°C/475°F/gas 9 and place a heavy baking sheet in the oven to heat.

Knock back the dough on a floured surface, roll into a 30-cm/12-in. round, transfer to a sheet of non-stick baking paper and, with wet hands, stretch the dough to your desired shape, pressing the top to form indentations. Spray or brush with water, scatter with nigella seeds, onion flakes and sea salt flakes. Drizzle over 1 tablespoon of olive oil, then slide onto the heated baking sheet. Bake for about 14–16 minutes until golden and cooked. Cool briefly, then serve drizzled with the remaining olive oil and black pepper.

MINI FLATBREADS
with spicy harissa & courgette flowers

20 g/¾ oz. tomato purée/paste

1 teaspoon harissa paste

2 teaspoons ground cumin

2 teaspoons ground coriander

2 tablespoons olive oil

100 g/3½ oz. cherry tomatoes, thinly sliced

½ quantity of Basic Flatbread dough (see opposite), brought to room temperature

flour, for dusting

1 pack courgette/zucchini flowers, stamens removed

1 courgette/zucchini, thinly sliced

10 mozzarella balls (optional)

MAKES 4–6 SMALL FLATBREADS

Put the tomato purée, harissa, cumin, coriander and olive oil in a mixing bowl. Beat well, then stir through the chopped tomatoes.

Take pieces of dough (about 150 g/5½ oz. each) and, using lots of flour, roll into a 15-cm/6-in. circle. Cover and leave for 15 minutes on a well-floured surface to allow the dough to relax.

Preheat the oven to 220°C fan/240°C/475°F/gas 9, or as high as it will go. Line a baking sheet with non-stick baking paper.

Roll the dough out thinly, to about 2–3 cm/1–1½ in. thick and place on the lined baking sheet. Divide the tomato mixture between each round of dough, spreading it right to the edge (use your fingers to spread it as this is much easier than using a spoon). Top with a courgette flower, courgette slices and some mozzarella, if using.

Bake the rounds, one at a time, for 4–5 minutes or until just beginning to colour. Remove from the oven and leave covered with a clean cloth to stop them drying out while you bake the remainder.

TOASTED & TORN FLATBREAD SALAD

6 long red peppers

1 teaspoon sumac

145 ml/⅔ cup extra virgin olive oil

3 heirloom tomatoes, quartered

2 large Basic Flatbreads (see left), made earlier

freshly squeezed juice of 1 lemon

1 tablespoon dried oregano, plus extra to serve

1 garlic clove, crushed

100 g/3½ oz. small stoned/pitted black and green olives

1 cucumber, shaved into ribbons

sea salt and black pepper

SERVES 4 TO SHARE

Preheat a barbecue to high or a char-grill pan over a high heat. Add the peppers and grill, turning, for about 10–12 minutes until well charred and softened. Remove from the heat into a bowl, sprinkle with sumac and drizzle with 1 tablespoon of the oil. Cool to room temperature, then split the peppers lengthways and discard the seeds and pith.

Brush the flatbreads with 2 tablespoons of the oil and grill for 2 minutes on each side until they are charred and crisp.

Whisk the remaining oil the with lemon juice, oregano and garlic in a bowl. Season to taste.

To serve, tear the flatbreads into pieces and arrange on a platter with the peppers, olives and cucumber. Drizzle with the dressing and scatter with extra oregano.

BLACK OLIVE & ROSEMARY SHARING BREAD

*This soft, enriched dough studded with olives makes the sharing bread.
It's perfect with a cheese board or a mezze platter, or served as a bread roll
with a meatball, pickled onion and tzatziki filling.*

300 ml/1¼ cups whole milk

1 tablespoon sea salt

140 g/scant ⅔ cup unsalted butter,
cut into cubes

2 teaspoons caster/superfine sugar

500 g/3½–3⅔ cups strong white
bread flour, plus extra for dusting

7-g/¼-oz. sachet of fast-action
dried yeast

1 tablespoon chopped fresh parsley

140 g/5 oz. black olives, stoned/
pitted and finely chopped

olive oil, for proving

sprig of fresh rosemary, leaves
picked

*20–23-cm/8–9-in. round cake
pan, lined with non-stick
baking paper*

SERVES 4–6 TO SHARE

Warm 80 ml/⅓ cup of the milk in a small saucepan over a low heat and add the salt. Stir to dissolve and set aside to cool.

Meanwhile, melt half the butter and all the sugar in 200 ml/generous ¾ cup of the milk in another saucepan set over a medium heat. Leave to cool until lukewarm.

Tip the flour and yeast into the large bowl of a stand mixer fitted with the dough hook attachment and mix together. Gradually work in the melted butter and milk mixture.

Once the dough begins to come together, add the salted milk, parsley and half the olives. Keep mixing for 6 minutes, or turn out onto a lightly floured surface and knead by hand for 10 minutes.

Oil a large bowl, add the dough, then rub oil over the top of the dough. Cover with a tea/dish towel and leave in a warm place to rest for at least 1 hour, or until doubled in size.

Meanwhile, heat the remaining butter in a small saucepan over a low heat and add the remaining olives. Set aside to cool.

Once the dough has risen, turn it out onto a lightly floured work surface and gently punch it back. Divide it into 8 pieces, between 130–140 g/4–5 oz. each, and roll them into tight balls, tucking the edges underneath so the balls are perfectly smooth with the seams on the underside. Arrange in the lined cake pan, ensuring the dough balls are equally spaced around the edge with one in the middle. Cover with a tea/dish towel and leave to rise for about 20–30 minutes until roughly doubled in size again.

Preheat the oven to 180°C fan/200°C/400°F/gas 6.

Brush the dough with some of the olive butter and scatter the rosemary over. Bake for 30–35 minutes until golden brown and cooked through. Pour over the remaining olive butter along with the olives. Serve warm.

SESAME BREAD RINGS *from Thessaloniki*

These are popular Greek street-food snacks – if you walk around Thessaloniki, you will see vendors selling them in piles on a stick. This version is a little softer than the street-food ones, and the bread rings look impressive piled high on a wooden board in a table, surrounded by dips and accompaniments.

300 ml/1¼ cups lukewarm water

7-g/¼-oz. sachet of fast-action dried yeast

1 teaspoon caster/granulated sugar

500 g/3½–3⅔ cups plain/all-purpose flour, plus extra for dusting

2 teaspoons sea salt

3 tablespoons olive oil, plus extra for oiling

200 g/1½ cups sesame seeds

MAKES 12 BREAD RINGS

Put the lukewarm water, yeast and sugar in the bowl of a stand mixer and stir. Cover the bowl well with clingfilm/plastic wrap and set aside for 8–10 minutes until the yeast starts bubbling.

Into the same bowl, add first the flour, then the salt and olive oil. Using the dough hook attachment, mix all the ingredients at a low speed for about 7 minutes until the dough becomes an elastic ball. When done, remove the dough from the hook, it should be smooth and elastic and slightly sticky.

Lightly coat a bowl with some olive oil, place the dough inside and cover with clingfilm/plastic wrap. Leave the dough to sit in a warm place for about 30 minutes, then knead the dough in the stand mixer again at medium-high speed for 3–4 minutes.

Turn the dough onto a work surface and divide into 12 pieces. Take one piece of dough and roll out into a rope about 35 cm/14 in. long. Form a circle and join the ends, pinching them together. Place the bread ring on a large baking sheet lined with non-stick baking paper and repeat with the rest of the dough.

Dip the bread rings in water and then in sesame seeds, making sure to cover them on all sides. Place them back on the baking sheet, leaving some distance between them. Leave them to rise in a warm place for about 30 minutes.

Preheat the oven to 180°C fan/200°C/400°F/gas 6.

Bake the bread rings in the preheated oven for 15 minutes until nicely golden brown and crusty.

dolcis

DESSERTS & CAKES

HONEY & RICOTTA SEMIFREDDO
with macerated cherries & strawberries

Semifreddo is different to ice cream or gelato as it's a frozen mousse with extra ingredients added for flavour. It has more air incorporated in the mixture, giving it the lighter feel. Ice cream is denser in texture, has a higher fat content and lower air content. This recipe is light as air with a mellow honey flavour and a pleasingly savoury tang from the ricotta.

oil, for greasing
300 ml/1¼ cups double/heavy
   cream
200 g/7 oz. ricotta
1 vanilla pod/bean, seeds scraped
grated zest of 1 orange
   (reserve the juice)
2 egg whites
60 g/2 oz. runny honey
40 g/scant ¼ cup caster/superfine
   sugar
30 g/1 oz. liquid glucose
80 ml/⅓ cup berry coulis

CHERRIES & STRAWBERRIES
200 g/7 oz. cherries, stoned/pitted
   and halved
200 g/7 oz. strawberries, hulled
   and sliced
100 ml/generous ⅓ cup dessert
   wine
60 ml/¼ cup runny honey,
   plus extra to finish
reserved juice of 1 orange
bee pollen (optional)

24 x 11-cm/9½ x 4½-in. loaf pan

SERVES 6–8

Brush the inside of the loaf pan with oil and line the base and sides with non-stick baking paper, leaving an overhang of about 2 cm/¾ in. (or use a silicone loaf pan).

Pour the cream into the bowl of an electric mixer and whisk until soft peaks form, then fold in the ricotta, vanilla seeds and orange zest. Transfer to a medium bowl and refrigerate.

Put the egg whites and a small pinch of salt in the clean bowl of an electric mixer with the whisk attachment in place.

Put the honey, sugar and glucose in a small saucepan over a medium-low heat and stir until the sugar has melted. Increase the heat to medium, bring to the boil and leave to bubble for about 2 minutes, resisting the urge to stir, until it registers 110°C/230°F on a sugar thermometer. Immediately begin whisking the egg whites on a high speed until soft peaks form. When the syrup reaches 116°C/240°F, remove the pan from the heat and turn down the mixer speed to medium. With the machine running, slowly and continuously pour the syrup into the egg whites, whisking all the time, until it is all incorporated, then continue to whip for another 8 minutes until the mixture is cool.

Fold in the whipped ricotta cream until completely mixed through, then pour the mixture into the prepared loaf pan. Ripple the berry coulis through to create a 'veined' effect and smooth the surface. Gently tap the pan on the work surface, transfer to the freezer and leave overnight.

Combine the cherries, strawberries, wine, honey and orange juice in a bowl, stir until well mixed, then refrigerate to macerate for 10 minutes.

Unmould the semifreddo on a chilled platter and serve in slices with the macerated cherries and strawberries, sprinkled with bee pollen if using.

PINK GRAPEFRUIT GRANITA
with caramelized citrus slices

Perfect as a palate cleanser or at the end of an indulgent dinner, this granita is refreshing and zingy. For added richness, serve with chilled custard drizzled over the caramelized citrus, or add a few shots of gin to the glass for a grown-up slushie.

800 ml/3⅓ cups pink grapefruit juice

200 ml/¾–1 cup elderflower liqueur

freshly squeezed juice of 1 lemon, strained

6 tablespoons caster/superfine sugar or to taste

gin, to serve (optional)

chilled custard, to serve (optional)

CARAMELIZED CITRUS SLICES

1 pink grapefruit, peeled and sliced into rounds

1 orange, peeled and sliced into rounds

1 clementine, peeled and slice into rounds

40 g/1½ oz. brown sugar

SERVES 4–6

Stir the grapefruit juice, elderflower liqueur, lemon juice and sugar together in a large measuring jug/pitcher or bowl until the sugar has totally dissolved, then strain the mixture into a freezerproof container. Put on the lid and place in the freezer for 2 hours.

Scrape the mixture with a fork to mix it up a little, then freeze again.

Repeat the scraping 2–3 times, every 1–2 hours, until the granita has a light, snow-like consistency.

For the caramelized citrus, arrange the citrus slices on a baking tray or heatproof platter. Scatter evenly with sugar and use a blowtorch for about 1–2 minutes to caramelize the surface of the fruit.

Spoon the granita into chilled glasses, add the citrus slices and serve immediately. If you wish, serve with a good sipping gin at room temperature and some chilled custard.

OLIVE OIL TORTA
with roasted stone fruits & vanilla

This soufflé-style cake is best eaten on the day of baking. It has a custardy texture flavoured with delicate olive oil and dessert wine, which pairs beautifully with the mellow vanilla and stone fruit. Drizzle with custard or simply eat on its own.

5 eggs, separated

grated zest of 1 lemon

100 g/½ cup caster/superfine sugar

60 g/2 oz. runny honey

1 teaspoon vanilla paste

125 ml/½ cup olive oil

125 ml/½ cup dessert wine

pinch of sea salt

½ teaspoon cream of tartar

150 g/generous 1 cup plain/ all-purpose flour

icing/confectioner's sugar, for dusting

ROASTED STONE FRUITS

100 g/½ cup golden caster/ superfine sugar

60 g/4 tablespoons runny honey

1 vanilla pod/bean, split in two, seeds scraped

freshly squeezed juice of 1 lemon

6 apricots, halved and stoned/ pitted

3 peaches, quartered and stoned/ pitted

3 nectarines, quartered and stoned/pitted

100 ml/generous ⅓ cup dessert wine

22-cm/8¾-in. round springform cake pan

SERVES 8

Start by making the roasted stone fruits. Preheat the oven to 200°C fan/ 220°C/425°F/gas 7.

Tip the sugar, honey, vanilla seeds and lemon juice into a pestle and mortar and mash together. Tip the fruit into a shallow baking dish, then toss in the vanilla sugar mixture and drizzle with the dessert wine. Add the vanilla pod to the dish. Roast for 20 minutes until the fruits have softened, but not collapsed and the sugar and fruit juices have made a sticky sauce. Set aside ready to top the torta.

Turn the oven down to 160°C fan/180°C/350°F/gas 4. Line the cake pan with non-stick baking paper and butter.

For the torta, whisk the egg yolks, lemon zest, half the sugar and all of the honey and vanilla paste in an electric mixer until thick and pale. Whisking continuously, add the oil in a thin, steady stream until emulsified. Gradually add the dessert wine, whisk to combine, then transfer to a large bowl and set aside.

Whisk the egg whites, sea salt and cream of tartar in the clean bowl of an electric mixer until soft peaks form. Gradually add the remaining sugar and whisk until stiff and glossy. Fold one-third of the egg white mixture into the yolk mixture to lighten, then fold in the remaining egg white mixture to combine. Sift over the flour and gently fold into the mixture. Pour into the lined cake pan and place in the oven.

Reduce the oven to 140°C fan/160°C/325°F/gas 4 and bake for 15–20 minutes until puffed and dark golden, then turn off the oven. Place a buttered round of baking paper on top of the torta, leave in the oven for 20 minutes, then remove and leave to cool in the pan. The mixture will collapse a little, but that's the nature of the cake – it's a little like a soufflé. Once cooled completely, remove the torta from the pan and place on a plate. Top with the roasted fruit with all the juices to serve.

COCONUT & SEMOLINA CAKE
with citrus syrup

*A simple revani cake is made all over Greece with a few variations. It is
really lovely with a mix of semolina and coconut and drenched with syrup,
making for a moist cake that is great served with Greek yogurt.*

100 g/1⅓ cups grated dessicated/
  dried coconut
5 eggs, separated
220 g/generous 1 cup caster/
  superfine sugar
300 g/10½ oz. coarse semolina
180 ml/¾ cup hot water
260 g/9½ oz. Greek-style yogurt,
  plus extra to serve
finely grated zest of ½ lemon
finely grated zest of ½ orange
80 g/¾ stick butter, melted, plus
  extra for greasing
plain/all-purpose flour, for dusting
  (substitute with semolina for
  a flourless version)

CITRUS SYRUP
300 g/1½ cups caster/superfine
  sugar
juice and thinly peeled rind
  of 1 lemon and 1 orange

23-cm/9-in. square cake pan

SERVES 6

Preheat the oven to 140°C fan/160°C/325°F/gas 3. Butter and flour
the cake pan and line with non-stick baking paper.

Scatter the coconut on a baking sheet and roast in the preheated
oven for 5–10 minutes until golden. Set aside until needed.

Beat the egg yolks and half the sugar in an electric mixer for about
5 minutes until pale. Combine the semolina and hot water in a bowl,
stir through the yogurt and lemon and orange zests and add to the
yolk mixture. Beat to combine, then leave to rest for 5–10 minutes,
before stirring through the melted butter.

Whisk the egg whites with a pinch of the sugar in an electric mixer until
soft peaks form. Whisking continuously, gradually add the remaining
sugar and whisk until the mixture is smooth and glossy. Fold this into
the semolina mixture until combined.

Pour into the prepared cake pan, smooth the top and bake in the
preheated oven for 45–60 minutes until golden and the centre springs
back when lightly touched. Cool in the pan for 20 minutes, then turn out
onto a platter and pierce all over with a skewer.

Meanwhile, make the citrus syrup. Bring the sugar, lemon and orange
juices and peel and 175 ml/¾ cup water to the boil in a saucepan, stirring
to dissolve the sugar. Ladle the syrup over the cake and leave to stand for
10–15 minutes until the syrup is absorbed. Scatter over the roasted
coconut and serve with extra yogurt.

GREEK-STYLE ALMOND BISCUITS
with orange blossom & ouzo

A traditional Greek kourambiethes is a shortbread-style cookie covered in icing/confectioner's sugar. Best served with a coffee and a cold glass of water, this version has a sprinkle of orange blossom and ouzo in the filling.

160 g/5½ oz. blanched almonds

300 g/2¾ sticks unsalted butter, softened

120 g/generous ¾ cup icing/confectioner's sugar, plus extra for dusting

1 egg yolk

60 ml/¼ cup ouzo, brandy or apple juice

1 teaspoon vanilla extract

1 teaspoon orange blossom water, plus extra to serve

450 g/3½ cups plain/all-purpose flour, sifted

75 g/¾ cup cornflour/cornstarch

2½ teaspoons baking powder

pinch of sea salt

MAKES 30

Preheat the oven to 160°C fan/180°C/350°F/gas 4. Line 2 baking sheets with non-stick baking paper.

Place the almonds on one of the lined baking sheets. Bake in the preheated oven, tossing occasionally, for 10–15 minutes or until toasted. Set aside to cool.

Place the almonds in a sealable plastic bag and use a rolling pin to crush them until they resemble coarse crumbs.

Meanwhile, use an electric mixer to beat the butter and icing sugar in a bowl until pale and creamy. Add the egg yolk, ouzo, brandy or apple juice and vanilla and beat to combine. Add the flour, cornflour, baking powder, salt and crushed almonds in batches, stirring after each addition until just combined.

Roll 2 tablespoonful portions of mixture into balls. Shape each portion into a crescent shape and place on the second lined baking sheet. Transfer to the fridge for 15 minutes to chill.

Bake the biscuits for 20–25 minutes until light golden. Place the extra icing sugar on a rimmed baking sheet. Transfer the biscuits to the baking sheet and roll in the icing sugar to evenly coat.

honey & honeycomb

Honey is an organic, natural sugar alternative with no additives, adapts to all cooking processes, and has an indefinite shelf-life. It is made by bees and stored in wax structures called honeycombs. Honey is used as a sweetening agent in a wide variety of foods including baked goods, beverages and more.

RAW HONEY This has not been filtered or pasteurized and thus contains the highest levels possible of flavourful and nutritious pollen.

UNFILTERED HONEY This is sometimes used as a synonym for raw honey, but more often it is used to refer to honey that has not been filtered.

ORGANIC HONEY Technically, organic honey means that the bees only pollinated organic flowers. In practice, it is impossible to track the behaviour of every bee.

PURE OR GENUINE HONEY This should mean 100 per cent honey which has not been adulterated with corn syrup, sugar or other ingredients. However, there is no governing body to enforce the use of this term, so always read the ingredients label to ensure you are buying 100 per cent honey.

SINGLE-SOURCE HONEY This means that the honey was made by pollinating only a single species of plant.

MULTI-FLOWER HONEY This means that the honey was made by pollinating multiple species of plants.

Honey is categorized into dark and light types.

DARK TYPES In general, the darker sorts have a stronger, more distinctive aroma. They not only taste less sweet, but are typically rather tangy with a bitter, malty note. In areas where flower nectar is not available, bees sometimes collect honeydew, the sugary metabolic product (or secretions) of specific scale insects that live on plants, or even invasive spotted lanternflies. This can be found on the pine needles or leaves of trees.

LIGHT TYPES Varieties of honey that are lighter in colour usually have a mild, floral flavour, and a colour that ranges from nearly clear to white, pale yellow, golden, orange or red.

Liquid, Whipped, and Honeycomb

Besides dark and light types, you can also differentiate between production processes. Most of what you will find available for sale belongs to the liquid nectar group, wherein the honeycombs are spun in a centrifuge to retain the actual product.

This liquid type is available in two varieties: raw or cold packed, and pasteurized. While the raw version includes pollen and minerals (particularly if it has not been filtered) and is therefore very popular, pasteurized sorts offer their own advantages, and they do not crystallize so quickly. As crystallization is a natural process, this is more a matter of personal preference. Also, it's important to keep in mind that most types do tend to crystallize over a certain time period anyway.

Pasteurization of honey is similar to the process used to make dairy products safer for human consumption, but it is not done for the same reason. Since honey is high in acid with a low moisture content, it doesn't provide a welcome environment for potentially harmful bacteria to thrive. Some types of yeast can sometimes survive, so pasteurization kills these, but as mentioned above, it mostly just helps to prevent crystallization.

The whipped variety provides a special texture, too. This type of processing is used when the honey already contains sugar crystals. By whipping in air, it will keep its smooth and spreadable texture over a longer period.

Comb honey is a true speciality, because it is sold in its original wax reservoirs, cut into pieces. This not only looks great, but it also offers you a direct connection with and experience of the natural product. Sometimes, you can find fluid versions that contain individual pieces of honeycomb, too.

DARK CHOCOLATE SORBET
with cardamon palmiers

Decadent chocolate sorbet with a cardamom palmier and served with a shot of amaretto for a match made in heaven – chocolate pairs beautifully with the herbal warmth of cardamom.

DARK CHOCOLATE SORBET

120 g/4½ oz. dark/bittersweet chocolate (64% cocoa solids), coarsely chopped

200 ml/generous ¾ cup milk

120 g/generous ½ cup granulated sugar

60 g/2 oz. liquid glucose

200 g/2 cups Dutch-processed cocoa powder

CARDAMOM PALMIERS

½ teaspoon ground cardamom

¼ teaspoon ground ginger

100 g/½ cup dark brown sugar, plus extra for dusting

1 sheet of ready-rolled all-butter puff pastry

20 g/1½ tablespoons melted butter

ice-cream machine

SERVES 4

For the dark chocolate sorbet, melt the chocolate in a heatproof bowl placed over a saucepan of simmering water. Combine the milk, sugar, glucose and 400 ml/1⅔ cups water in a saucepan and bring to the boil. Whisk in the cocoa powder. Cool slightly, then pour this onto the melted chocolate, stir and churn in an ice-cream machine following the manufacturer's instructions. Freeze until required.

To make the palmiers, combine the spices and sugar in a bowl. Lightly dust the work surface with sugar. Roll out the pastry to 3-mm/⅛-in. thick, then cut out a 30-cm/12-in. square. Brush the pastry lightly with melted butter, scatter the spiced sugar mixture evenly over the top, then roll the 2 sides inwards to meet in the centre. Transfer to a baking sheet and refrigerate until firm.

Preheat the oven to 200°C fan/220°C/425°F/gas 7. Line one or two baking sheets with non-stick baking paper.

Slice the rolled pastry into 1-cm/½-in. thick pieces and place on the lined baking sheets, leaving about 5-cm/2-in. gaps in between each. Bake, swapping and turning the baking sheets partway through to cook evenly, for about 5–6 minutes until lightly golden. Remove from the oven, carefully flip the palmiers over, then return to the oven and bake for a further 2–3 minutes until the bases are glazed and caramelized. Leave to cool and serve with a scoop of the chocolate sorbet.

HONEY & PISTACHIO BISCOTTI

Also known also as cantucci, biscotti are Italian almond biscuits that originated in Tuscany. However, this more-ish recipe uses pistachios for a different flavour, and the honey brings a mellow sweetness. Dipping them in dark chocolate takes them to another level.

oil, for greasing
200 g/1½ cups pistachios, shelled
130 g/4½ oz. honey
100 g/½ cup butter, softened
100 g/½ cup caster/superfine
   sugar, plus extra for rolling
2 eggs
2 tablespoons orange juice
finely grated zest of 1 orange
350 g/2⅔ cups plain/all-purpose
   flour
1½ teaspoons baking powder
150 g/5 oz. dark/bittersweet
   chocolate for dipping

MAKES 25

Preheat the oven to 150°C fan/170°C/325°F/gas 3. Lightly oil a baking sheet and line another 2 sheets with non-stick baking paper.

Dry-roast the pistachios in a small frying pan/skillet over a medium heat until golden and fragrant. Add 80 g/3 oz. of the honey and cook until caramelized. Spoon onto the oiled baking sheet and leave to cool completely, before breaking into small pieces.

Use an electric mixer to beat the butter, sugar and remaining honey in a large bowl until pale and fluffy. Add the eggs, orange juice and zest and beat to combine. Stir in the flour, baking powder and the caramelized pistachios (reserving 50 g/½ cup to decorate) and mix to combine.

Divide the mixture in half and, on a heavily sugared surface, roll each half into a 30-cm/12-in. long log. Place each log on one of the lined baking sheets and bake until golden. Remove from the oven and transfer to a wire rack to cool completely.

Thinly slice the logs and arrange the slices on the other lined baking sheet and return to the oven. Bake for about 8–10 minutes until lightly golden, turn and bake for another 8–10 minutes until golden and firm to the touch. Leave to cool on a wire rack.

Place the melted chocolate in a bowl and dip the biscotti into the chocolate just to half coat. Place onto a wire rack and sprinkle with the remaining chopped pistachios. Allow to set and devour!

These will keep for up to 1 month stored in an airtight container.

WALNUT & ESPRESSO CAKE

A favourite afternoon pick-me-up or a great cake to serve to a crowd.
Incredibly moist and tasty with the classic combination of coffee and
walnut, this will become a family favourite.

220 g/generous 1 cup golden
 caster/superfine sugar

4 eggs, separated, plus 1 extra
 egg white

130 g/1 cup walnuts, finely
 chopped, plus extra to finish

100 g/¾ cup plain/all-purpose
 flour, sieved

sea salt

ESPRESSO CREAM

100 g/¾ cup pure icing/
 confectioner's sugar, sieved

100 g/1 stick softened butter

30 ml/2 tablespoons espresso

100 g/3½ oz. dark/bittersweet
 chocolate, melted

22-cm/8¾-in. round cake pan

SERVES 6

Preheat the oven to 160°C fan/180°C/350°F/gas 4. Line the cake pan with non-stick baking paper.

Whisk the sugar and egg yolks together in an electric mixer for about 4–5 minutes until very thick and pale and the mixture resembles frosting. Transfer to a large bowl, stir in the walnuts, then the flour, a little at a time, until combined (the mixture will be very stiff).

Whisk the egg whites and a pinch of salt in an electric mixer for about 2–3 minutes until firm peaks form, then stir half of this into the walnut mixture. Fold through the remaining egg white and spoon into lined cake pan.

Bake in the preheated oven for 20–25 minutes until lightly golden and firm to touch. Cool in the pan, then turn out, trim the sides and cut in half horizontally.

For the espresso cream, beat the sugar, butter and espresso in an electric mixer for about 6–8 minutes until pale and fluffy. Swirl the melted chocolate through the cream. Spread the bottom half of the cake with half the espresso cream, sandwich with the top half and set aside to set for 20–30 minutes.

To serve, pile the remaining espresso cream on top and scatter with extra chopped walnuts.

SUMMER RASPBERRY TARTS
with almond pastry

Classic almond pastry and crème pâtissière topped with raspberries that are then glazed – nothing looks more elegant. The perfect end to a celebratory summer meal, these look and taste lovely served with chilled pink Champagne or other sparkling rosé wine, such as Crémant.

ALMOND PASTRY

200 g/1½ oz. plain/all-purpose flour

175 g/1¾ cups ground almonds

175 g/scant 1 cup golden caster/superfine sugar

200 g/1¾ sticks cold butter, diced

1 egg yolk

100 g/3½ oz. dark/bittersweet chocolate, melted

CRÈME PÂTISSIÈRE

150 ml/⅔ cup whole milk

1 teaspoon vanilla paste, or seeds scraped from 1 vanilla pod/bean

25 g/1 oz. caster/superfine sugar

25 g/1 oz. plain/all-purpose flour

1 egg, beaten

75 ml/⅓ cup double/heavy cream

TOPPING

4 tablespoons raspberry jam/preserve

450 g/1 lb. raspberries

sprigs of Greek basil, to decorate

6 x 10-cm/4-in. individual tart pans

MAKES 6

Make the pastry by tipping all the ingredients, except the egg yolk and chocolate, into a food processor and pulsing to the texture of breadcrumbs. Add the egg yolk, then pulse until it all comes together to form a soft pastry. The pastry will be too soft to roll out, so press it evenly into the tart pans until the pastry comes up above the edges. Transfer to the freezer to rest for at least 20 minutes.

Preheat the oven to 170°C fan/190°C/375°F/gas 5.

Line the tart cases with non-stick baking paper and fill with baking beans, then place on a baking sheet and bake for 10–15 minutes until the edges are starting to brown. Remove the beans and paper, then continue to cook for 5–7 minutes until biscuity. Leave to cool, trim the edges with a knife, then carefully remove from the tarts from the cases.

Meanwhile, melt the chocolate and brush the tart cases with melted chocolate, then set aside to set.

To make the crème pâtissière, put the milk and vanilla in a saucepan set over a medium heat. Heat until it is just scalding and you are just able to dip your finger in. Put the sugar, flour and egg in a mixing bowl and whisk together. Pour in half the hot milk and whisk until smooth, then pour in the remaining hot milk. Pour the mixture back into the saucepan and cook over a low heat, stirring all the time, until very thick, about 2–3 minutes. Pour into a bowl, cover with clingfilm/plastic wrap and chill in the fridge until cold. Once cold, pour in the cream, while whisking constantly. Spoon the crème pâtissière into the tart cases and chill in the fridge for about 1 hour until completely cooled.

To make the glaze, heat the jam in a saucepan with a tablespoon of water and whisk to combine. Strain the liquid through a sieve into a small bowl. Arrange the raspberries standing upright on the crème pâtissière and brush the warm glaze over the top. Decorate with sprigs of Greek basil and serve.

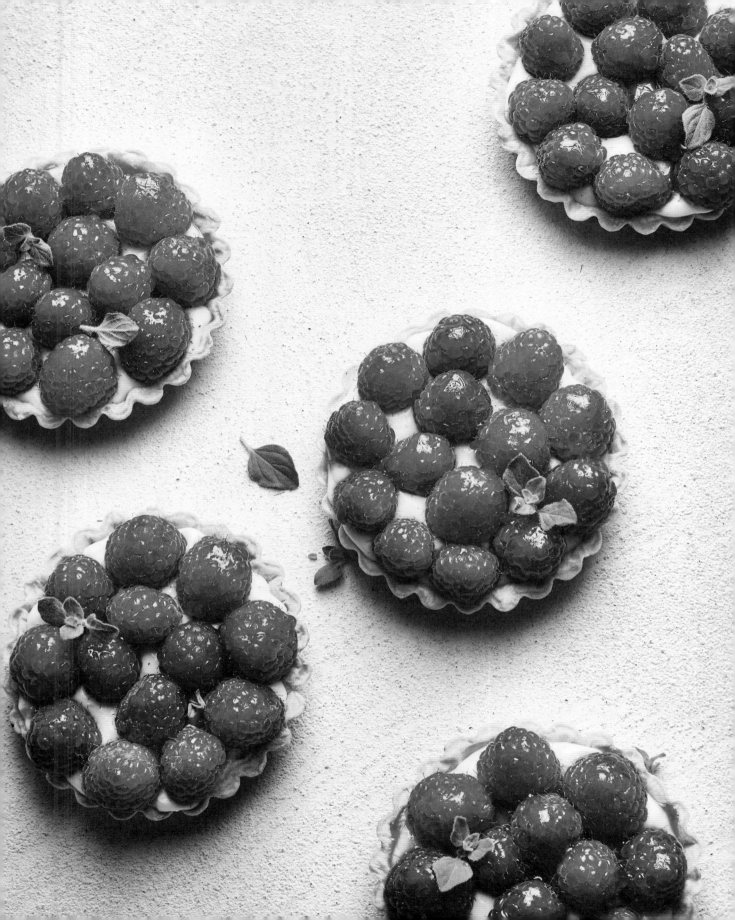

INDEX